The Apprentice's Tale

The Apprentice's Tale

By Hugh Mackay Ross

Watson & Dwyer Publishing Ltd.
Winnipeg, Manitoba

Watson & Dwyer Publishing Ltd.,
232 Academy Road
Winnipeg, Manitoba R3M 0E7

Canadian Cataloguing in Publication Data

Ross, Hugh Mackay
   The apprentice's tale
   Includes index.
   ISBN 0-920486-14-2 (bound). — ISBN 0-920486-16-9 (pbk.)
   1. Ross, Hugh Mackay.   2. Fur traders — Ontario — Biography.
3. Hudson's Bay Company — Biography.   4. Fur trade — Ontario —
History — 20th century.
I. Title.
FC3075.1.R6A3 1986   971.3′103′0924   C86-091447-X
F1058.R6A3 1986

Cover: Jane Allyn Ross

Printed in Canada by
Hignell Printing Limited
Winnipeg, Manitoba

DEDICATION

In Memory of Beatrice Dingle Ross
who died in October 1966
and to our children
Barbara, Jennifer, Dorothy and Ian

Acknowledgments

I am indebted to Alex Ross of the Hudson's Bay Company Archives, Provincial Archives of Manitoba, for his assistance in verifying facts and figures.

I also thank my wife, Jane Allyn Ross, who consistently urged me to get on with this story, and who, once I had begun, encouraged and supported me by typing and retyping, proof-reading and editing the manuscript.

Hugh Mackay Ross
Winnipeg, July 1986

Author's Note

During my years in the bush a man was known as either a Treaty Indian (or Indian) or a half-breed, either of Scottish or French descent. Half-breed was an honourable term. The people were proud of their heritage. I know this from personal experience, for I met many of them all over the North: McKenzies, McDonalds, McLeods, McCallums, Rosses and Linklaters.

The métis, I always understood, were half-breeds of French and Indian ancestry, living in the Red River Settlement. I did not encounter this term until 1948 when I first visited Green Lake in Northern Saskatchewan. Here the provincial government had gathered together a group of displaced half-breeds into a farming community and referred to them as métis. Perhaps the government was right, as many of the Green Lake settlers were descendants of the followers of Louis Riel and Gabriel Dumont who had fled the Red River Settlement.

To my mind the word half-breed is a correct and honourable term. I never heard the term 'mixed-bloods' during my years in the northern bush.

This book has been published with the help of grants from the Canada Council and Manitoba Arts Council.

CONTENTS

This Agreement, made this _Nineteenth_ day of

April A.D. 19 _30_ .

Register No. _____ Form No. 1.

Between _Hugh M Ross_

of _Station Road Rothes_

in the County of _Elgin_ hereinafter called "the party of the first part," of the first part

and _William Craighead. agent of_

the Governor and Company of Adventurers of England Trading into Hudson's Bay, commonly called
The Hudson's Bay Company, hereinafter called "the Company," of the second part.

1. The party of the first part, for the consideration hereinafter mentioned, agrees to enter into the
service of the Company and to serve the Company at such place or places in North America as the
Company or its officers shall direct, in the capacity of Apprentice and in such other capacity as the
Company or its officers shall from time to time appoint, for the full term of five years, to be computed
from the date of embarkation to Canada A.D. 19 ____ and for such further term as is hereinafter provided;
and that he will, during the whole of such time, diligently, honestly and faithfully serve the Company and
perform all such work and services for the Company as he shall be required and directed to perform by
the officers thereof, and abide by all rules and regulations now or hereafter made by the Company and
applicable to his employment.

2. That he will not (during the period of his engagement hereunder) engage nor be concerned
either directly or indirectly in any trade or employment whatsoever except for the benefit of the Company
and according to its orders, and that all goods obtained by barter with the Indians or otherwise which
shall come to his hands or into his possession or within or under his control or direction shall be held or
controlled by him for the Company only and shall duly be delivered up to the Company, its officers or
agents.

3. The party of the first part further agrees with the Company that in case he shall not give at
least twelve months previous notice in writing of his intention to quit the service of the Company at the
end of the said term of five years (which notice shall be given to the officer in charge of the post where he
then is, or in the event of his being himself in charge of a post, then to the officer in charge of the district
where his post is) he shall remain and continue in the service of the Company for the further period or
term of twelve months after the expiration of the term above agreed upon, on the terms and conditions
herein contained.

4. The Company hereby agrees with the party of the first part that in consideration of the services
to be rendered and performed by him, the Company will, during the time that he shall remain in the
service of the Company, pay him at the rate of $240 for the first year, $300 for the second year, $360 for
the third year, $420 for the fourth year, $594 for the fifth year, to be computed from the day of
embarkation A.D. 19 _30_ .

It is further agreed that of the above sums the Company may retain in each year an amount not
exceeding 25% of the total payable in that year until such time as the cost of transportation of the party
of the first part from the United Kingdom to Canada has been refunded.

Upon the satisfactory completion of the term of service set forth in this Agreement, the amount so
retained will be returned by the Company to the party of the first part.

The Company will also provide for him board and lodging according to the usual custom of the
Company's service, or will at the Company's option pay to him such additional sum per month in lieu of board
and lodging and all allowances as shall be from time to time fixed and allowed therefor by the Company.

5. Provided always and it is hereby expressly agreed between the parties hereto that it shall be
lawful for the Company or its officers at any time during the said term or any extension thereof to
terminate this Agreement by giving to the party of the first part ninety days previous notice in writing or
at the option of the Company on payment by the Company to him of three months wages in lieu of notice.

In witness whereof, the party of the first part and the Company have executed these presents

at _Aberdeen_ on the _19_ day of _April_ 19 _30_ .

Witnessed by _David Mitchell_

Hugh M Ross (Apprentice)

Address _Victoria Hotel, Forres_

J Sutherland

Craighead (For the Hudson's Bay Co.)

Address _Commercial Bank Maud_

Approved _Annie Mackay Ross_ Parent (or Guardian).

Registered _____

Chief Accountant. (Winnipeg)

Approved _____

Secretary.

Date of Birth _March 24. 1912_ Place of Birth _Rothes_

Married or Single _Single_

Where last employed _Elgin & District Bus Coy._
Elgin

Hugh Ross's five-year contract with the Hudson's Bay Company.

ILLUSTRATIONS

Photographs are from the collection
of H. M. Ross unless otherwise
stated.

MAPS
Maps are by Caroline Trottier
of Winnipeg.

FOREWORD

In the 1960s when I worked at Hudson's Bay House, Winnipeg, the Canadian Headquarters of the Hudson's Bay Company, I frequently sought out Hugh Ross for help in answering the numerous historical inquiries I received. He was well informed, eagerly shared his knowledge, had an irreverent wit, and seemed to be unaware that he belonged to an unusual group of men who are part of fur trade history.

June 1930 was not the most propitious time to join the Hudson's Bay Company, but Hugh Ross, fresh from Scotland, arrived in Northern Ontario that summer for his posting to Grassy Narrows. He travelled all day by canoe with two Indians, making eight portages, wearing his blue double-breasted suit and pointed brown oxfords. One longs to know what the Indians thought of this latest recruit.

In his second year, Ross was sent as manager to Long Legged Outpost, a three-day canoe trip from Grassy Narrows. As the Indians spent most of their time hunting, his only companions were a dog, the field mice, and his violin. Ross's relationship with the Indians was one of mutual respect. His statement that 'unless they were in contact with white people they were utterly dependable' is an unflattering legacy for many Canadians.

Ross served under the legendary Fur Trade Commissioner Ralph Parsons. Parsons' concern, interest, and personal intervention into the domestic arrangements at Grassy Narrows for Ross's bride add another dimension to that man.

Part of the book belongs to Beatrice Vivian Dingle, who married Hugh Ross in September 1935. Like so many fur traders' wives before her she was an unusual woman, living in the bush 'in always less than elegant accommodation, without seeing another white woman for months at a time.' The events surrounding the impending birth of their first child in 1939, including the canoe and jumper sleigh transport to Temagami village, are filled with anxiety, universal understanding of the father's behaviour, and finally gratitude for another life.

This autobiography is written with clarity and humour, retaining some of the expressions of the 1930s. Ross's detailed descriptions of the trade goods, including brand names and prices, the habits of the Indians and the Saturday night dances at Minaki Lodge will be of special interest to students of fur-trade history, and native and women's studies.

We build our memories on every day events. I am grateful to Hugh Ross who, in the 1960s, shared many of his memories with me, as I endeavoured to learn about the Hudson's Bay Company. He has now made them available to a wider audience. We are all richer.

Shirlee Anne Smith, Keeper
Hudson's Bay Company Archives
Provincial Archives of Manitoba.
August, 1986

1

SCOTLAND: 1930

'Can you ride a bareback horse?'

The question took me by surprise. I was being interviewed by a panel of four men, headed by Dr Alex Milne, a retired employee of the Hudson's Bay Company: David Mitchell of Forres and Charlie Stephen of Aberdeen, two Hudson's Bay post managers who were home in Scotland on furlough; and Mr William Craighead, a banker from Maud who was the Company's representative in the north-east of Scotland.

The date was 19 April 1930. I was eighteen years old and scared to death.

I suppose the depression of 1929 and a magazine notice were responsible for my being in this small office building on Market Street in Aberdeen. Lots of people think that the depression was a strictly American disaster but it had world-wide repercussions, affecting even the small town of Rothes where I was born.

It was a small, sleepy town, nestled in the valley of the river Spey and considered by those in the know to be one of the finest salmon-fishing rivers in the world. Its sole industry was the production of Scotch whisky and most of the 1,200 inhabitants worked in one of the four distilleries within the bounds of the town itself or in any one of several more in the area. Nowadays, it is part of the 'Whisky Trail' and popular with tourists.

My father, Richard Ross, was born in the Black Isle in Rosshire. He joined the Seaforth Highlanders' Battalion of the regular army at the age of 12 as a boy piper and saw active service in Egypt and the Sudan; later, he took part in the Boer War. On being discharged, he worked in the northern part of Scotland where he met and married my mother, Annie Mackay of Altna-breac, Caithness. Her forebears were of the Mackays of Strath-naver who had been evicted during the Highland Clearances in the nineteenth century.

During World War I, father worked as a woodcutter in the forests of Speyside, being too old for active service. After that he settled down in Rothes and worked as a maltman at the Glen Grant Distillery. Officially the workmen were issued one free drink of whisky per day, but they had their own special device for securing further supplies. The men in the local coppersmith's shop fashioned copper cylinders about 13 inches long and one inch in diameter; which the workmen hid in their trousers, hanging by a string from their braces. They called it a 'plumper', and whenever an opportune moment presented itself, they pulled the cylinder out from the trousers, dropped it down into the bung-hole of the whisky barrel and, quick as a wink, returned it back inside their pants.

The depression had the whisky business in the doldrums. Each year the active distilling season became shorter and shorter and the distilleries were closed and silent for longer and longer periods. When this happened, father managed to find some kind of work. I suppose we were poor but we didn't realize it, as we always had plenty to eat. Mother had a large garden which produced lots of vegetables and, on top of this, father was an inveterate poacher.

At an early age, he introduced me and my older brother Dick to this gentle art. On many a dark night, Dick and I were stationed in secluded spots to watch for the water bailiff while father took a salmon from a pool in the Spey with a torch and gaff.

If he knew for sure that the bailiff was going to be off his beat, father had another method which was more productive but definitely louder. He placed some carbide — used to light bicycle lamps — in a bottle, partially filled it up with water, capped it and threw it into a salmon pool. Then we stepped back, waiting for the water to react with the carbide and BOOM! The bottle exploded in the pool, stunning the salmon which rose belly-up on the surface. We carried them home in poacher's pockets at the back of our jackets or hanging down inside our pant leg. We ate well on salmon for several days.

Another of father's methods for keeping the larder full was 'bolting' rabbits. Again, Dick and I had to keep watch this time for the gamekeeper, while father placed nets over all the bolt holes and then put our two pet ferrets down the rabbit holes. He was adept at this and I only remember him getting caught once; this resulted in a fine to him and a cuff on the ear to Dick and me, with a warning to keep a better watch next time.

After finishing primary education at the Rothes School, I went on to Elgin Academy and in March, 1929, sat for my university entrance examinations or, as it is known in Scotland, my 'Higher Leaving Certificate'. I hoped to get my degree at Aberdeen University and become a teacher of English and Classics. Although I did win a few small bursaries, it quickly became evident that there was no way I could afford to stay in residence at the university or in digs in Aberdeen. So I had to get a job and within a week of sitting for my exams, I was working as a bus conductor for the Elgin and District Bus Company, commonly known as the Grey Line which ran between Elgin and Aviemore.

Today, Aviemore is a bustling ski centre, but in 1929 it was just another wee town up in the Cairngorm Mountains. The bus stopped at each and every village and hamlet. Sunday was our busiest day. By law, you had to be a bona fide traveller in order to buy a drink at a pub on the Sabbath. So we would pick up a busload of people at one town, carry them the required three miles to the next town and thus they were bona fide travellers, able to quench their thirst. After closing hours, the procedure was reversed. This was only a temporary job and in the autumn, I was laid off. The following winter was a difficult one. Not just for me; the depression affected everyone.

I had thought of getting a position as a bank clerk or in a solicitor's office but this would have called for my parents to make a premium payment of £50.00 to £75.00 to my employers, which they simply could not do. Like so many others, I went on the 'dole'. In those days, in order to collect money from Social Assistance, you had to report to the dole office each day. All available jobs were listed on a large blackboard, the first job listed was yours and you took it or you got no money. So that winter I went from one odd job to another: digging gardens, hoeing turnips and cutting peat for use in the distilleries. This went on for months and I could see no way forward. My older sister Isobel had emigrated to New Zealand and my brother Dick had joined the regular army and was serving with the Seaforth Highlanders on the Northwest Frontier in India.

Early in January, 1930, I was sitting in the reading room of the local men's club, looking at a magazine called *Canada*. At the back, in the 'Answers to Correspondents' column, I came across an interesting reply which gave the address of the head office of the Hudson's Bay Company in London. They apparently hired on a regular basis a number of apprentices in the Old Country and sent them out to Canada on a five-year contract to learn the fur trade. I read it through a couple of times, copied down the address and hurried home to dash off a letter.

In reply, a letter arrived from the Secretary of the Company, Chadwick Brooks. We carried on a correspondence for most of that winter, during which time I supplied character references from my local headmaster, the Elgin Academy headmaster, and our minister; as well as medical and dental certificates.

That winter I was fortunate to meet James McGibbon who had come home to our neighbourhood on holidays after having spent considerable time with the Company, most recently as manager of the post of Fort Chimo in Ungava. My conversations with him only whetted my desire to go to Canada. Eventually I received a notice from Chadwick Brooks to proceed to Aberdeen for a personal interview.

So here I was, pondering the question 'Can you ride a bareback horse?'. I had never been on a horse in my life. The previous question 'Can you steer a course by the stars in an open boat?' was much easier to answer. My Boy Scout training saw to that. I thought fast. How could they check out my answer if I said 'yes'? What could they do? There were more than fifty hopeful and nervous young men in the office to be interviewed. Maybe the Company had a horse, minus saddle, tied up outside the building in the middle of Aberdeen and planned to take each of us out in turn to ride the animal. No, I thought, they wouldn't go to all that trouble. Besides, I didn't think they had horses in the Arctic. So I confidently answered, 'Yes sir, I can ride a bareback horse.'

After checking over my credentials and references, they sent me back to join the others. As each of us returned to the group, we compared notes on what kinds of questions were being asked.

'But I can't ride a horse,' one lad blurted out. 'Surely they wouldn't turn me down just for that, would they?' I wondered whether I should tell him how I had answered that question but decided to keep my own counsel.

After what seemed like hours, Mr Craighead came out to us, called out twenty-five names and told us to go into the next room. We wondered what would happen next. Would they tell us that we should try again next year? I wasn't very confident and as we waited, I contemplated another year of working at odd jobs. My sister Isobel wanted me to come out to New Zealand. She said it was much like Scotland.

Then the door opened and Mr Craighead informed us that we were the fortunate candidates. He produced an official look-ing document, asked us to read it over carefully and then sign it. This contract was for a five-year period, in which we promised to serve the Hudson's Bay Company and no one else, for the princely sum, I thought, of $240.00 per annum for the first year, rising annually to a maximum of $504.00 in the fifth year. This, of course, included our room and board. I signed the contract and thus became a member of 'The Governor and Company of Adventurers of England Trading into Hudson's Bay'.

Once Mr Craighead had collected all the contracts and left the office, pandemonium broke out. We clapped each other on the back, congratulated each other and went out to celebrate.

I arrived home in time for tea. When I announced that I had been accepted by the Company, mother said, 'Well, it looks like all my children will be scattered all over the globe.' Dorothy, my younger sister, asked what Canada was like, but before I could answer, mother said, 'Cold! I had better get on with knitting you some warm socks.'

I pushed the food around on my plate waiting for my father to say something. Finally he looked up at me sternly and said,

'Mind you don't bring home an Indian princess for a wife.'

Two months later, I bade goodbye to my family, my fiancée Peggy, and all my pals, and boarded the train to London with a suitcase in one hand, which contained my worldly possessions —most of them books I had won as school prizes — and my violin in the other.

In London, we gathered at Hudson's Bay House where we were entertained for a day and met the rest of our party, comprising in all forty-four budding apprentices: twenty-four from Scotland and twenty from England.

On 19 June 1930 we sailed from Liverpool on the *Duchess of Bedford,* travelling tourist class. None of us had ever been on an ocean liner and once we were on the high seas, most of us spent the first couple of days suffering from seasickness. I quickly got my sea-legs and enjoyed this new experience.

During the voyage, daily sessions were held in the first-class lounge, giving us a brief glimpse of how the upper classes lived on shipboard. Mr James R. Drummond-Hay and Mr George Binney, who were in charge of our group, advised us on what to expect in the job and encouraged us to ask any questions we had. Messrs Mitchell and Stephen, the two post managers who were returning to their posts, must have thought some of the questions daft. One chap from Peterhead stood up and asked in his broad Buchan accent, 'And what if I'm up in the Arctic and have an appendix attack? What happens then?'

Forty-four heads turned expectantly to Mr Binney. He peered over his glasses, looked at the lad and in a deep voice replied, 'You die, my boy. You die.'

That was the end of the question period for that day.

When we docked in Montreal, Jerry Wilmot, the Company's representative, met us, quickly sorted us into groups and gave us our railroad tickets and letters of instructions. With the exception of twelve boys who stayed behind, he saw us all off on the westbound train to our various destinations. To our minds, the twelve were the fortunate ones. They were going to the Arctic and were awaiting the sailing of the Company's ship *Nascopie* from Montreal.

Once the train was underway, I opened the envelope of

instructions and discovered I was to get off at North Bay, Ontario, which I did, along with three other chaps in the party. At the Company's District Office there, two of these lads — M. S. Cook and James E. Holden — stayed behind. W. S. Franklin and I caught the westbound train the next day, finally getting off at the small settlement of Hudson, Ontario where we reported to Harry Woods, the post manager. My travelling companion was an Englishman and he immediately struck it off with Mr Woods who was also English. He was invited to assist in the office while awaiting the boat going north to his post at Lac Seul, while I was assigned the task of swabbing the floor and tidying up the warehouse. Two days later, I caught the local train to a point in Western Ontario called Jones Station.

Jones Station was a tiny place. The bush and rocks closed in on it from the north and a large lake stretched out towards the south. I was the only passenger to get off the train. There wasn't a soul about. I guessed that it was only about seven in the evening so I decided to have a look around. Beside the small railroad station there was a large tower which, I later learned, provided water for the locomotives; a couple of cottages, and what looked to me like the bunkhouses I had seen in the illustrated stories of the American West. Despite the fact that the weather was warm, the evening beautiful, and I was full of anticipation, I couldn't help feeling a bit disappointed at the lack of a reception. I sat down on my suitcase and waited, not knowing what to do next.

A long time passed and then I heard the sound of a motor boat chugging slowly across the lake. As I walked down to the shore, a skiff pulled up and four men got out, carrying rods and a full string of assorted fish. One of them introduced himself as Mr Willett, the telegraph operator who was in charge of this lonesome station. I gathered he was a bachelor. He didn't invite me into his house but allowed me to go into the waiting room where he handed me a cup of tea through the wicket. It didn't look as if I was going to get any supper so I sipped the tea very slowly. When I finished Mr Willett took the cup and said, 'Well, young fella, it don't look like that canoe from Grassy Narrows is gonna arrive tonight.' He reached under his cap to scratch his head, sighed and said reluctantly, 'I suppose I'd better find you a place to sleep.' I gathered up my suitcase, violin and a brown paper-wrapped parcel containing a 4-point Hudson's Bay blanket which Mr Woods at Hudson had insisted I would need. It was charged up to the Grassy Narrows expense account. I followed Mr Willett down to the bunkhouse where he told me the section men slept when they were working on the railway. He pointed to a bunk, said good night and left. I looked around the room. Mattresses were stacked one upon the other in one corner. As I picked up the top one, several field mice scurried to find cover. The place smelled musty and there were droppings everywhere. I didn't dare get undressed, so I wrapped myself in the blanket and spent a rather uncomfortable and hungry night wondering why I had ever left Scotland.

Next morning was bright and clear. There was no wind and within minutes after I emerged from the bunkhouse, a canoe paddled by two men came around the point and pulled in at the station dock. This was my canoe and the two Indians had been sent down from Grassy Narrows to fetch me. They were nice enough looking chaps; with their weather-darkened skin, they reminded me of tinkers — the men who travelled the country roads in Scotland patching pots and pans. They were the first Indians I had ever met. With the exception of the odd word, they didn't seem to speak any English at all, or perhaps my Scottish accent sounded like a foreign language to them. They smiled cheerfully, stowed my belongings in the canoe and we were on our way.

At the first portage they stopped to make breakfast and never was I so happy to get something to eat. Pork and beans and salt pork, all heated together in the frypan, whetted my appetite. I had as much as I wanted and a large mug of tea, sweetened with condensed milk, added the finishing touch. We travelled north all day, making eight portages in all. I must have looked a strange spectacle, walking across the portages behind the two Indians, in my double-breasted blue suit, of which I was very proud, and my pointed-toed brown oxfords.

Late in the afternoon, as we crossed Delaney Lake, the wind began to come up. When we crossed the portage to Grassy Narrows Lake, we were faced with the long arm of the lake; whitecaps were rolling down it at a great pace. It was apparent that we couldn't travel in this rough weather, so the Indians cooked another meal and we sat waiting for the wind to go down. They left me to my own devices, so I wandered a little way from the camp-fire — but never too far away — and had a look around. Just as it was getting dark, the wind dropped and we got under-way again. About an hour later, we rounded a point and there in the gathering darkness, was the bulk of a large island with two or three white buildings.

I had arrived at Grassy Narrows.

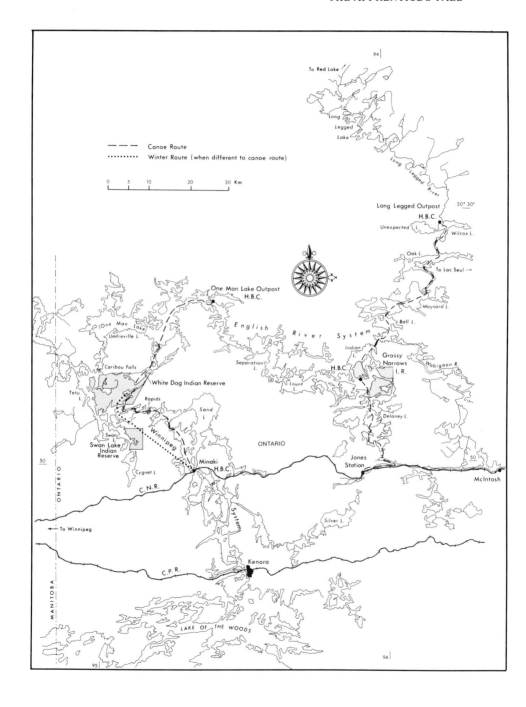

2

GRASSY NARROWS: 1930-31

Early next day I was up and about to explore the new home that I had been too tired to see when we arrived. Grassy Narrows is part of the English River system which flows through a series of lakes from Lac Seul in Northern Ontario west to the Manitoba-Ontario boundary where it joins the Winnipeg River and enters Lake Winnipeg near Fort Alexander. The post was built on a large island about eleven acres in size and roughly the shape of a whale's hump. The mainland around the lake constituted the Grassy Narrows Indian Reserve. All the houses where the Indians lived were built on the north and east sides which were flat and meadow-like, hence the name. The rest of the mainland was rocky, covered with beautiful stands of spruce and jackpine trees. There was a large number of small, tree-covered, rocky islands dotting the surface of the lake, very reminiscent of Scotland to me.

The post consisted of a log dwelling house, a trading store and two small warehouses; these were arranged roughly in a square, right on top of the island which had been cleared of all growth as a fire protection.

Around the island there were many clumps of birch and poplar trees, and alder and saskatoon bushes. On the eastern end there was a small beach. The dwelling house was beautifully constructed of squared logs dovetailed at the corners; the spaces between the logs were filled with lime plaster.

The roof was covered with large, square, tin shingles of a variety I had never seen before or since. These were about a foot square and interlocked in such a way that they were completely waterproof. And, of course, they were a great protection against fire. Inside, the house was divided into four rooms: living-room, bedroom, kitchen, and an office that was also used as a bedroom. The walls were lined with beautiful tongue-and-groove pine which, unfortunately, was painted with canoe enamel in strange colours of crimson, grey and green. The houses were heated by a large iron heater shaped like a barrel and long enough to take four-foot logs. It stood in the middle of the living-room and was only lit during the winter.

The same type of heater was in the store, a storey and a half framed building. The outside walls were covered with a heavy rubberoid — a type of roofing — and painted white; the Hudson's Bay Company sign in old English lettering hung above the door. The two small warehouses were built of logs, and had flat, sloping roofs, just like sheds. All the buildings were white with dark green trim around the windows and doors. The roof and doors were painted red. These were the standard Company colours that were used at every post.

After breakfast, I handed Mr Murchison, the post manager, the letter of introduction with which I had been provided at District Office. He read it slowly, stuffed it in his pocket and then spoke to me in a language I didn't understand. I looked at him in surprise. Did he expect me to know Indian? Then in English, he asked, 'You don't have the Gaelic, do you?' When I answered in the negative, he snorted. 'Humph! A hell of a fine Scotsman you are.' And that was me, catalogued.

Donald Murchison was born in Stromeferry in the North West Highlands. He joined the Company as a labourer at Stromness in the Orkney Islands in 1884 and sailed from there directly through Hudson Strait into James Bay. He saw service at various posts including Abitibi and Grand Lac. During this time, he was promoted from labourer to store assistant and eventually to post manager. He ended up in charge of Nemaska where he stayed for many years, then moved south to the charge of Nipigon House. En route to Nipigon House, he saw and rode in a railway train for the first time in his life. He had been at Grassy Narrows for a few years and was getting close to retirement age.

Mrs Murchison, his second wife, was an Indian woman from Nipigon House. They had three daughters: two teenagers and one

HBC Archives, PAM

Donald Murchison, post manager at Grassy Narrows, with his younger son, Kenneth, c. 1925.

HBC Library

Grassy Narrows Post: from the left, the trading store, warehouse and dwelling house. c. 1929.

about twenty-four; an older son, Johnny, and a young son about twelve named Kenneth. The oldest daughter, Mary, had two children, born when she was in her teens. The family spoke Ojibway in the house all the time, except when they had to speak to me. I was always puzzled about how or where they all slept, because they all crowded into the one bedroom at night, with the exception of Johnny who slept in his sleeping bag on the living-room floor.

That first breakfast was really strange. The boss and I sat at the table in the living-room and were waited on by his family, who afterwards ate separately in the kitchen. This was to be the normal procedure during my stay at Grassy Narrows. Donald rarely left the island or, in fact, the house. The only trip he made every day was down to the shore to feed the sled dogs. Other than that, he went to the store only when a customer appeared. On these occasions he put on his official Hudson's Bay hat — a sort of naval cap, the type called a 'cheesecutter'. It had a red enamel Hudson's Bay flag badge in front, surrounded by gold leaves. This had been the official cap introduced by a previous fur trade commissioner. An apprentice clerk wore a plain cap with only a flag; a post manager's had the flag and gold leaves; and a district manager's cap had a flag, gold leaves and a bunch of scrambled eggs — gold braid — as well. I never did have one of these caps, and shortly afterwards their use was discontinued.

Mr Murchison was a peculiar man. He walked up and down the living-room of the house for hours, never saying a word. He must have done this for years, because the linoleum where he walked was worn bare. He had two favourite expressions. One was 'It will be all the same a hundred years from now' and the other, 'Don't mind the expense; it's coming off a broad back.'

Johnny, the elder son, had been sent to Kenora the previous fall. In an effort to give him a good start in life, his father had bought him a complete set of mechanic's tools and had got him a job in a garage to learn the trade. When spring rolled around, however, Johnny got itchy feet and sold all the tools. He bought himself a second-hand canoe and paddled all the way back from Kenora. He did nothing all summer other than mingle with the natives playing poker. In the winter, he ran a wintering outpost called Long Legged Outpost which was open from October to the end of May.

The Murchison girls were kept very much under their father's thumb, possibly as a result of Mary's early pregnancies. They were not allowed to go anywhere by themselves. If a canoe party showed up, the girls were shooed into the house; then Donald would meet the visitors, talk with them and sell them any goods they wanted from the store. But he never invited anyone into the house. He wanted the girls to make good marriages but how they were to meet anyone suitable was beyond me.

Even I was not immune from Donald's suspicions. Any time I walked around the island, I was shadowed by little Kenneth or the boss's sled dog, Caesar, and I knew Donald was not too far behind. It got to be quite a game. Each time I went out of the house I knew I was being followed, so I would wander all around the island, glancing backwards for the occasional glimpse of a young boy or a black and white dog.

Every two months or so Donald would have a case of whisky sent in from Kenora. Then he would start drinking, a tumbler of half whisky and half water, every half-hour for as long as he could stand up. Then he went to bed — but the same glass had to be brought to him every thirty minutes until there was only half a bottle left.

On one occasion when he was drunk, he lined up his daughters and told me to take my pick. His wife grabbed a broom, shook it in my face and said, 'Just you dare.' Since he never mentioned it when he sobered up, I don't think he remembered the incident at all.

The trading store was a new world to me. A large heater sat in the centre of the floor, with long serving counters running along each side of the store. Behind each counter were rows of shelving filled with trade goods. A stairway ran up one wall to the attic where extra stocks of dry goods and hardware were stored neatly in rows. This attic was also used to hold the furs we purchased from the trappers in the winter. The skins were strung in bundles and hung on nails from the rafters. The fur baling press was kept in the space under the stairs.

Our customers were the Ojibway Indians from the Grassy

Narrows Reserve. At that time there would be about 80 families — men, women and children, numbering close to 300 people in all. The dry goods and groceries in the store were ordered with their needs and preferences in mind.

The grocery department was on the left-hand side of the store. There was lard in one-pound packages and three, five, and ten-pound pails. Lard was the mainstay of the Indians and they used it instead of butter. They could eat as much as a pound a day of it. Their systems seemed to crave it, for there was little fat on the carcasses of the deer that they shot. Baking powder for making bannock stood next to parcels of salt and tins of black pepper.

There were rows of canned fruit — peaches, pears and pineapple; followed by canned vegetables — tomatoes, sweet corn, peas, and Clark's pork and beans, the staff of life in the North. One-pound tins of Wagstaff's assorted jam stood next to Lyle's Golden Syrup. Tea, in one-pound and half-pound packages, stood next to Eagle Brand condensed milk.

The tobacco section held tins of plug tobacco — McDonald's Briar Plug tobacco and Prince of Wales chewing tobacco — and a brand of fine-ground tobacco that was generally known to the traders and the Indians as Copenhagen 'snuff'. I hadn't heard of this snuff before, but apparently the Indians couldn't live without it. They might have to do without tea, but if they had to go without snuff for a day, they actually became sick. They did not take it by delicately sniffing it up a nostril, as I had visualized snuff being taken in the Old Country. Men, women and children stuffed it between their lips and gums, both upper and lower. I thought it a disgusting habit, especially the incessant spitting that accompanied it. There were also a few packets of fine cut tobacco and Zig-Zag cigarette papers; this was how the cowboys I had seen in the silent movies used to roll their cigarettes. I tried it out and made a mess of it at first, but soon I got the hang of it. When I ran out of tailor-mades, I could roll my own with the best of them.

The bottom shelves held ten-pound bags of sugar, six-pound bags of rolled oats and 25-pound boxes of sweet biscuits and dried fruits — raisins, apples and prunes. The dried fruit was used to make home brew. It was against the Company policy to sell yeast cakes to the Indians but they always were able to get supplies of this at the railroad track. So the brew kettles were always on.

Under the counter were large barrels containing bulk supplies of white and brown sugar, corn meal, rice and navy beans. All bulk goods were weighed out on the old fashioned beam scale that stood on the counter. Matches were kept under the counter in a metal-lined box — a precaution against fire, the scourge of the North. There was a barrel of hard-tack biscuits, which were used as a substitute for fresh bread. These biscuits were rock hard but very sustaining, especially when smothered in strawberry jam and washed down with lots of strong, sweet tea.

The last section of shelving contained drugs and candy. There were various liniments such as Perry Davis's Pain Killer; Minard's Liniment and Eclectic Oil. We had to be extremely careful in selling patent medicines to the Indians, as it was contrary to the Indian Act to sell them anything containing alcohol. We had pills for everything: Carter's Little Liver Pills, Gin Pills which caused the urine to turn green and delighted the Indians, Beecham's Pills and Dodd's Kidney Pills. And, of course, aspirin.

With the exception of 'Oh Henry' and 'Sweet Marie' candy bars, chewing gum and 'Cracker Jack', all our candy was in bulk. Christmas hard candy mixture was a favourite, along with hard Scotch mints and jelly beans. It was seldom that an Indian traded in the store without buying some candy for his children.

Across on the other side of the store were the dry goods and hardware sections. The dry goods were mainly various types of cloth, which the women bought by the yard to make up their own dresses. Prints in floral patterns of reds, blues and greens were the favourites, especially among the younger women. The older women were conservative and usually bought 'Magog', a better quality print, which came in navy or black with a small, white floral-spray pattern and sold at 50¢ per yard. Prints and flannelette sold at three yards for $1.00; and Galaplaid, an all-wool tartan material sold at $2.50 a yard and was mostly used to trim babies' cradles or *tikanagans,* as the Indians called their infant carriers. Coloured strouds and 'Superfine' cloth, very expensive, were sold for trimming mukluks. Factory cotton,

unbleached cotton and cheesecloth were bought to make mos-
quito nets. The bottom shelves held grey flannelette sheets,
quilted comforters and bolts of canvas duck. This duck came in
various weights from six to twelve-ounces and was used for
everything from making tents to re-covering canoes.

The women's section was spartan. Underwear consisted of
fleece-lined bloomers; hosiery — brown lisle stockings for
summer and black worsted stockings for winter. Headgear
consisted of Basque berets, bright woollen toques and brightly
coloured satin head squares. For the older women, there were
black cashmere fringed shawls. Heavy jumbo-knit wool sweaters
served for both men and women but the women's had sailor
collars and the men's, rolled shawl collars.

In the men's wear, we had Penman's wool socks in various
weights from two and a half to five pounds; and brown cotton
gloves and woollen mitts to be worn under deerskin mitts. We
carried no wool underwear — it was too expensive — only the
fleece-lined kind, and mostly in separate shirts and drawers, with
a few pairs of combinations for the customers who were more
modern. Black or blue denim overall pants were the order of the
day, with a few pairs of bib overalls. These were normally carried
in sizes 40, 42 and 44. If a trapper wanted a smaller size, he bought
a size 40 and his wife took in a tuck at the waist. Denim jackets
were worn in winter to break the wind, with a cotton shirt underneath. In summer, the men wore light-coloured Donegal tweed
caps and in winter, navy blue or black melton caps with fur-lined
earbands.

From the ceiling beams hung sneakers or running shoes,
which the young people bought in the summer, and moccasin
rubbers, the universal footwear. These moccasin rubbers were a
sort of flat overshoe which slipped over deerskin moccasins. They
were worn summer and winter and were slipped on and off when
going outdoors or coming in. They kept the feet dry whether in a
canoe or walking in the snow.

In the notions department were rolls of brightly coloured
satin ribbon of various widths, used as hair ribbons and to deco-
rate dresses or cradles. There were barrettes and bobbie pins;
black and white thread in various sizes; and needles, glover's

Unidentified Ojibway women wearing jumbo-knit wool sweaters with sailor collars. Grassy Narrows Treaty Day, 1936.

Unidentified Grassy Narrows family dressed for Treaty Day: dresses from a floral print, Donegal tweed cap, satin headsquare and sailor sweater.

Winter attire won by Tempen Skatchay Keesik (6'2"): melton cap, Penman's woollen stockings, cotton shirt, moccasin rubbers.

needles and sewing machine needles. The glover's needle had a sharp, three-cornered point and was used in sewing deerskins. For decorating moccasins, we had skeins of embroidery silk and a large selection of coloured seed beads. These were small, round beads which came in strings and were made in Czechoslovakia.

The hardware contained ammunition, of course, mostly 30.30 and 44.40 calibres which were the popular weapons, along with 12-gauge shotgun shells and .22 shells. There were all sizes of sheet tin and retinned pails with bailed handles which were used for cooking, mainly because they could be hung over an open fire.

Fry-pans, enamel mugs and tin plates stood next to tin basins and milk pans. There were assorted files, butcher knives, awls, gimlets and crooked knives — an indispensible tool for shaping canoe paddles or snowshoes; copper rivets and burrs for mending harnesses mingled with one-ounce rolls of brass rabbit-snare wire and 16 and 20-strand coils of cable snare wire for foxes and wolves. The lower shelves held Gilling twine, 16 one-ounce balls to the packet for sewing moccasins or making fish nets; and hanks of seaming and backing twine, also for fish nets. There were skeins of No. 7 and No. 9 twine for making snares and hanks of codline for lashing toboggans.

Under the counter were boxes of Victor steel traps for trapping anything from an ermine to a beaver. Next to them sat kegs holding nails of all sizes, from shingle nails to eight-inch spikes, and rolls of sheet-metal stove pipes, stove elbows, roof jacks and dampers.

One warehouse held cases of groceries, including our flour supplies in 24, 49 and 98-pound sacks. Flour was shipped in heavy canvas bags to protect the fragile cotton sacks from damage when being carried over portages. This was called Osnaburgh packing. The heavy canvas bags were greatly sought after by the Indians who used them for patching their tents and canoes. There was also a huge pile of 'D.S.B.' — dry salt bellies — pork in jute sacks. The Indians loved it and bought it at every opportunity. It helped to satisfy their crying need for fat.

One end of the other warehouse held roofing and building paper. There were rolls of heavy brown or green Kraft building paper for lining the interior of log houses, and light tarpaper or heavy slate roofing for covering the roofs. The other end held the relief supplies from the Department of Indian Affairs. Every month the old people came over to collect their ration of flour, baking powder, salt pork, tea, salt and navy beans. These stocks were shipped in by Indian Affairs; we stored and distributed them at no cost. The first of each month was always a busy day until all the old-timers had received their rations.

A small shed apart from all the other buildings held our coal-oil. This came in two four-gallon tins to the case, for ease in portaging. In winter, it was difficult to pour out coal-oil, as, in extremely cold weather, it thickened to the consistency of molasses.

*   *   *

After the boss had shown me around, I asked him what my duties would be. He told me that there was no future in learning to be a post manager. If I really wanted to get on in the Company's service, I should be an accountant and to do that, I must learn to do the books. 'This is a great opportunity for you,' he said. 'The Company has started a new system of bookkeeping. I don't know anything about it and you may as well take it over and be the bookkeeper at this post.'

The new set of books and forms were in the office (which also served as my bedroom), along with detailed instructions on how the system was to operate. I didn't know anything about keeping books. Before I left the Old Country, I had questioned my schoolmaster on this subject and he advised me that the most common system of bookkeeping was double entry and each different company had its own system of doing it. The main thing to remember was that wherever there was a debit, there had to be a credit in another account in the same amount and when the totals in all accounts were added up, they should balance. I read the instructions carefully, studied all the examples which were attached and soon got the hang of it.

The former system of bookkeeping had been a cumbersome one. All the transactions in the store were written up in a book called the 1-10 Day Book. It was divided up into ten columns and each individual transaction was written up, whether it was cash, barter, furs purchased, transfer to expenses or whatever. The amount was entered into the total column and also in each of the 1-10 columns provided in the book. At the end of the month, these columns were all added up and the various entries from each column posted to the control ledger. After this was done, a series of forms numbered FT 1 - FT 10 had to be filled out individually and from them a trial balance and a trading account was struck off. These were then forwarded by the first outgoing mail to District Office.

Under the new system, counter slip books were used in the store and transactions were entered into a daily list of sales form and the cash book or fur-purchase book, whichever was applicable. The individual customer's debits and credits were posted daily to the accounts in the customer's ledger. The forms were all in duplicate and at the end of the month, I added them up and forwarded them to District Office where the accounting department completed the work and sent back a trading statement. I found the system simple to operate and was soon doing what little bookkeeping was required at that time of year. The only thing I didn't like was that at the end of each month, form FT 75 had to be filled out which listed each customer's old debit balance, current amount of credit, current amount of fur purchased, current debit balance, and adding the old debit balance I got the total amount of debt the individual owed. This was a long, boring business and had to balance to the penny.

By late spring most of the local Indians had gone down to a town called McIntosh on the railroad track where their children attended the Indian school, so there was little business in the store. In McIntosh, they picked up odd jobs — worked on the railroad, picked blueberries or went fishing. They did anything to earn a living and often had a tough time of it until the winter came on and they were able to trap again. At that time there were no Family Allowance cheques and no Old Age Pensions for native people.

The few people who stayed around the reserve set their nets daily and lived on the fish they caught. They traded the odd fish to us at 25¢ per whitefish and the women made moccasins which we bought for $1.00 a pair. In the winter we sold them back for $1.25. Later in the fall they harvested the wild rice which we bought at 10¢ a pound and then sold back to them in the winter at two pounds for 25¢.

Remembering the fine meals we had eaten at home in Scotland, I was appalled at the food served at Grassy Narrows. We had whitefish, boiled or fried, practically every day, all summer long. In the fall, we got a few ducks and in the winter, rabbits. I used to enjoy a dinner of rabbit back home where they fed on grass, but these bush rabbits lived mainly on willow bark and were tough and bitter-tasting. Even today, I can't look at whitefish or rabbit on the menu.

If an Indian came in and said he was going out to hunt deer, we gave him two shells which cost about 10¢ each. If he was successful, he would bring a leg of venison to us and keep the rest of the meat for himself. So the venison was charged to the mess account at a cost of 20¢.

There was no bread. Mrs Murchison made the traditional Indian bannock, which was close to a sort of Scottish scone, made with flour, water, baking powder and salt; sometimes she threw in a few raisins.

Since we had no garden at the post, we had no fresh vegetables and no potatoes. Occasionally we had a can of peas or corn or tomatoes but instead of potatoes, the staple was white navy beans. These dried beans had to be soaked overnight, parboiled and then put into the oven to bake with several strips of salt pork laid over the top. I rather liked them but not for every meal. There were times when I would have given anything for a good boiled potato.

The depression affected the Hudson's Bay Company too and operations were being tightened up. A new fur trade commissioner, Ralph Parsons, had been appointed and he was determined to make things hum. All posts were given four years to make a trading profit — a profit on their merchandise sales after all expenses had been deducted. Up until this time, merchandise had been considered simply as a means to an end. The merchandise was kept on hand to obtain fur on which we could make a profit. But now, each post had to at least break even on trading and any profits on furs were an additional boon. If any post couldn't bring this about in four years, the post would be closed down. Quite a few posts were closed as a result of this policy. I gathered that the ruling also applied to district managers. Their districts had to make a trading profit or else.

This was one reason, perhaps, why our diet at Grassy Narrows was so austere. In addition, all other expenses were closely controlled and no repairs or improvements of any description costing more than $5.00 could be carried out at the post without written confirmation from District Office.

There was so little to do during the summer that I got bored. I tried to help with the chores but was politely told that it wasn't my job. I was the apprentice and not the choreboy. I couldn't carry up any water from the lake or bring in or split any wood. Years later, when I went back to Grassy Narrows and read through the old correspondence, I found the explanation for this. In my letter of introduction, District Office had stated that, while I was expected to do my share of the work, I was a trainee to learn the business and I was not to be treated as a choreboy. In his own peculiar fashion, Donald Murchison had written back, acknowledging receipt of the letter and stating that, in his opinion, it would be a small operation indeed that could not afford to keep one 'gentleman' and he saw no reason why Mr Ross should not be the gentleman at Grassy Narrows.

I revelled in the continuing hot summer weather. We had nothing like this in Scotland — day after day of bright sunshine. Unfortunately, I discovered mosquitoes about the same time that they discovered me. The midges of Speyside I had put up with but those Canadian mosquitoes were sheer torture. I must have tasted particularly succulent to them because they attacked me every time I went out. My face, neck, arms, and ankles were masses of red blobs which I tried vainly not to scratch. I suffered badly from them that first summer but strangely, never again in all the years afterwards.

Down by the beach there were three large 'Lac Seul' freight canoes. These were used for hauling in our annual freight each fall. There was also an 18-foot canoe which we used on the monthly trip down to the railway track for the mail. I asked the boss whether I could take the canoe out on the lake but he refused me, with the explanation that there was a letter on file stating that no apprentice clerks were allowed to go out in canoes until they knew how to paddle. I suppose this instruction was well meaning, but for the life of me, I couldn't see how I was going to learn to paddle a canoe on dry land. Finally I got a few trips around the island with one or the other of the Indians who had brought me across originally. But it was a year before I learned how to handle a paddle properly and mastered the subtleties of steering.

Four miles south of us, at the other end of the portage into Delaney Lake, was a fire rangers' cabin where three rangers were stationed. Each summer they manned a tower and kept a continual watch for any outbreak of fire. They did not, as a rule, come to visit the post because they knew they would not be welcomed by Mr Murchison. One day, in passing, they saw me on the shore and pulled in. From then on they came frequently and took me for rides in their big canoe with a fine outboard motor. On one or two occasions, they took me down to the cabin to spend a few hours with them. I enjoyed their conversation as much as the good meals they prepared.

About the beginning of September, the Indians began to drift back from their tents along the track near McIntosh to the reservation, and soon it was time for the annual supplies to be freighted in. The boss had sent out the necessary requisitions for the year's supplies earlier on, with instructions that the railway freight car be spotted at Jones Station on a certain date. Eighteen natives were hired, as it took six to handle each canoe — four paddling amidships, one bowman, and one steersman. They were paid at the rate of $5.00 per day, plus their board. It took them roughly twelve days to bring all the supplies back.

The freight was paddled across each lake in turn, then portaged over to the next lake; if the weather turned, the whole operation was hung up and the men sat around eating. They were not given any rations for this trip but simply helped themselves from the merchandise they were bringing in. When they arrived back at the post, all the freight was checked into the warehouse and the store from the bills of lading. Any groceries not accounted for, such as pork and beans, jam, tea and lard, were assumed to have been used for mess supplies and were charged up to the freighting account.

Invoices covering all this merchandise arrived at the same time. Then followed a hectic week in which all the invoices had to be cost-landed and the goods marked. The invoices stated the weight and number of each carton and the contents, and whether they were shipped first, second or fourth class by rail. To the invoices we attached aprons which were ruled in columns and from our list of tables, we added the required railway freight rate, railway insurance, and a percentage of the total wages and messing costs. Thus we arrived at the landed costs at the post. Then a percentage profit was added and a selling price fixed. In later years, this laborious practice was discontinued and all invoices were worked out on machines in the depot office in Winnipeg. When the invoices were received at the post, they were already complete with the cost-landed price. It eliminated an enormous amount of time and we knew exactly what to sell the goods for the minute they were received.

Practically the only exception to annual freight was the Copenhagen Snuff. This came in twenty-four rolls to the case, eight tins of snuff in each roll. In those days, the snuff was not vacuum-packed and shelf time was limited. The Indians objected to buying stale snuff and to overcome this difficulty, several cases of snuff were ordered each month; these were brought in by the mail canoe in the summer or by the mail team in winter.

By October the men started to talk about going to their traplines and came over to the store to find out how much advance credit or 'debt' they were going to get that particular winter. We made sure that they did not spend it foolishly, but first bought flour, tea, baking powder, tobacco, lard, ammunition and traps, so that they would be properly equipped. Day by day, families drifted away in their canoes, loaded down with their dogs and gear, all heading north to the cabins on their trapping grounds, until most of the people on the reserve were gone. There were always a few who stayed behind. We called them 'pot-hunters'. They stayed around the main post all winter and didn't extend their traplines beyond a few days' travel from the reservation.

District Manager S. J. C. Cummings, an Aberdonian, on inspection tour. Grassy Narrows, October, 1930.

Young Johnny Murchison was the last to leave. He had two freight canoes loaded with supplies for the winter at Long Legged Outpost which was situated about forty miles north of the parent post and roughly halfway to the trapping grounds. It was intended to serve as an intermediate station for the Indians who would come there to trade their furs and replenish their supplies. Mainly this was done in an effort to keep them from coming all the way back to the main post where they might decide to carry on down to the track and trade their furs to an opposition trader, in which case they were likely to 'forget' to pay the debt we had advanced to them.

One October day we were surprised to see an airplane approaching the island. It circled around once or twice, made a landing on pontoons and came right up onto the beach and docked. It was the first airplane I had seen close up. I think it was a Gypsy Moth with an open cockpit, owned by Western Canada Airways based at Sioux Lookout.

When the passenger alighted, we found it was our district manager, S.J.C. Cummings, on a quick inspection tour of his district. He didn't stay long, as the pilot was anxious to get back. Other than shaking hands and passing the time of day, I didn't see much of him. He spent an hour or so with Donald Murchison and from the sound of things, Cummings was not at all pleased. He certainly tore a strip off Donald, citing everything from lack of sales to too high expenses. Most of this I heard from where I was sitting on the outside steps of the store. Cummings made no bones about his feelings and left in high dudgeon. Poor Donald was not the same for days.

*   *   *

As October rolled on, I enjoyed my first sight of thousands of Canada geese flying south, and the magnificent panorama of leaves turning to red and gold. By early November the leaves had disappeared from the trees and the island looked bare.

Soon ice was forming along the shore and, bit by bit, it spread outward until, at last, the whole lake was frozen over. About a week after this the Indians began cautiously feeling their way across from the reserve to the post, tapping the ice with sticks or axes and telling by the resulting sound whether it was strong enough to walk on. At first they had to make many detours, as there was quite a strong current where the main force of the river flowed from east to west. But gradually the ice thickened up and it was safe to walk on anywhere. I had never seen ice like this and by mid-January when it was frozen three feet deep, I was amazed. I felt sorry for the boss's daughters who had to chop holes through this depth of ice with an ice chisel to get all the water that was required for the household.

In late December we were able to send the first dog-team down to the rail line for mail. When it arrived back, I betook myself to my room until I had read all my letters and glanced through all the local Scottish newspapers my mother sent to keep me up with what was happening at home. This was the time when I felt really homesick.

There was not much work to do. I had read all the books that I had brought with me two or three times over, including all the works of Shakespeare and Milton. To this day, I can still quote whole sections from most of Shakespeare's plays. It grew dark by four o'clock and the house was lit by coal-oil lamps. I soon learned to say 'coal-oil' and not paraffin.

There was a gramophone in the living room and about a dozen records with such heart-stirring titles as *Abdul, the Bulbul Amir, Big Rock Candy Mountain* and *The Prune Song.* I used to play them sometimes as a diversion but this didn't please the boss and one day the winding handle of the gramophone disappeared. He had locked it in the safe — so no more music. There was, of course, no radio. I kept my fiddle in the store and spent hours playing it there so that I wouldn't disturb any of the family.

After supper each night, I retired to my room, lit my lamp and read. I read the local Scottish newspapers from cover to cover, including the 'for sale' ads and the obituary notices. Then I kept them and read them again. I knew what was going on in Scotland but I didn't have a clue as to what was happening in Canada or the rest of the world. We never received any Canadian newspapers.

Now that the freeze-up had arrived, my days of isolation on the island were at an end. Michell Keesik, our Ojibway handyman, introduced me to the art of snow-shoeing. And what an introduction it was! My legs ached for the first week or so, but my muscles soon toughened up and I was able to handle the snow-shoes with ease. At first I must have looked like a duck as I tried to waddle along with legs apart, but I soon learned to roll as I moved and slide one snow-shoe over the other. From then on, it was easy.

The Ojibway snow-shoe is made with a high curve in the front to enable the shoe to clear itself easily from the snow. I soon found out that, with snow-shoes, one did not walk on top of the snow, but rather sank into it from six to eight inches depending on the depth of snow. The snow-shoe bindings were made of lampwick. These bindings had to be adjusted exactly so that they fitted across the toes; then they were looped through the snow-shoe mesh and tied behind the ankles, leaving just enough of my toes to stick through the hole in the webbing to give me a grip when going uphill. But my feet could not be too far forward or they hit on the wooden crossbar.

A couple of white fishermen had come up from the railroad track and established themselves on the lake about two miles from the post to carry on a winter commercial fishing operation. I got to know them quite well and walked over on the weekends to visit. These outings were all faithfully recorded in the post's *Daily Journal of Events:* 'Mr Ross left to visit the opposition at 3 p.m. and returned at 8 p.m.' or whatever. One of the men was an Icelander who knew the technical side of the business and the other was a young Englishman named Joe Green, the nephew of a Mr Wilcox who ran a trading store at Canyon Lake. Joe played an excellent banjo and we had many pleasant times together until they returned to the railway track just before break-up.

It was time for our dog-team to go to work. There were four dogs, all black and white collies and good workers. Four was the usual number — any more were useless when travelling through the bush. The wheel or lead dog was usually bigger and more powerful than the other dogs, as it had to break the toboggan loose when the command to 'mush' was given. The lead dog did little actual hauling but was most valuable in its ability to answer the driver's commands and to follow the trail if it was covered by newly fallen snow. The only fault with our collies was that the snow tended to form hard balls between their toes, freezing in their long hair. If this was not caught in time and the iceballs pulled out, their feet were liable to bleed.

The usual load was four hundred pounds of freight or one hundred pounds per dog. There were only four commands: 'Gee', 'Haw', 'Mush', and 'Whoa'. The driver talked to his dogs all the time and the more interesting his conversation, the faster the dogs went. The driver carried a dog whip — a five or six-foot lash on a one-foot handle. This he cracked to make a fearsome noise, but I seldom saw a dog driver actually hit his dogs unless they got into a fight or got snarled up in their harness.

The dog harness was made of two leather traces attached to a padded collar which slipped loosely over the dog's head. All the pulling was from the shoulder. A back strap and a belly band held the traces in place. At the top of the collar were standing irons and these usually were decorated with streamers of ribbon or large woollen pompoms. Most drivers had a strap of bells attached to the backstrap, which jingled merrily as they went along.

I had the usual romantic notion of skimming across the snow by dog-team, closely wrapped in a fur rug and ensconced in a cariole, but these illusions were soon shattered. With a working team, I did little riding unless I was travelling empty.

The Ojibway toboggan was built specifically for use in the bush and was a marvellous piece of work. It was made from two planks, roughly seven and one-half or eight inches wide and approximately ten feet long. The planks were usually maple or birch and were less than half an inch thick. This enabled the whole toboggan to bend up and down when crossing portages between lakes or going over deadfalls.

The first three feet of the toboggan were steamed and bent in almost a complete circle, something like the scroll of a violin. Then both front edges of this upward curve were tapered in, so that the toboggan would bounce or glide off any obstruction on the portage without capsizing. When loading, a tarpaulin was spread over the toboggan and the load was placed on it so that the centre of gravity was kept low. Then the tarpaulin was folded over and the whole thing was cross-lashed. An axe, indispensible when travelling, was slipped underneath the lashings.

The grub box was stashed at the front, along with the tea kettle and the kettle for boiling the dog food. A tow rope about eight feet long was attached to the rear of the toboggan. This was used as a steering rope to guide the dogs around obstacles on the portage. At first, I used this rope for more than steering. The dogs went at a steady lope — too slow for a run and too fast for a walk and I'm afraid that I occasionally hung onto the steering rope in order to keep up with the dogs.

With a full load, I was either dog-trotting behind the toboggan or walking ahead of the team on snow-shoes, breaking trail. If the snow was deep, I sometimes had to double track ahead in order to beat down a proper path for the dogs.

On starting out first thing in the morning, it seemed that each dog had to defecate. Not all at once — but one after the other. If I didn't keep an eye open, whenever a dog made a motion to step aside on the trail, I had, at best, a mass of dogs tangled up in their harness; or at worst, a toboggan that had run over the defecation. Then I would have to stop, turn the toboggan on its side, scrape the bottom clean again with an axe, right the toboggan and give it a heave to get the team in motion once more. After this was done three or four times when hauling a full load, it got rather tiresome.

In early December, I made my first dog-team trip out to the track along with Michell Keesik. Just before freeze-up, my tonsils had started to give me trouble and were now inflamed and swollen. Before I could go out to see a doctor, I first had to get permission from District Office to leave the post. We had no radio telephone, so by the time the boss had written a letter to Winnipeg, freeze-up was on and I did not get the necessary permission until the first winter mail. I caught the train at Jones Station, where I would be met by the dog-team two weeks hence.

When I arrived at Sioux Lookout, a divisional point on the railway, I went to see the doctor. There were two doctors in the town: Doctors Bell and Day who jointly ran the drugstore. After a brief examination, I was sent over to the hospital. The last thing I remember seeing before I went under was Dr Day standing in the middle of the operating room in his Stanfield long johns. When I came out of the ether, I had a couple of forceps sticking down my throat and was most uncomfortable. After a week in hospital, I hung around town for a further week before the doctor pronounced me ready to return to Grassy Narrows. I made the most of my time in town, talking to people and eating everything except whitefish. And potatoes with everything!

Just before Christmas all the trappers came back from the trapping grounds and we were busy trading in the store. I saw mink, otter, foxes, lynx and fisher for the first time and watched the boss closely as he graded and bought the furs. He did not attempt to teach me any of the required skills of fur buying. After the furs had been bought, the amount of the trapper's debt was subtracted from the total. My job was to sell as much of this credit balance as I could in merchandise, so that little cash changed hands. Of course, we had to give some cash to the few Indians who brought in fairly large catches but this was the exception; there didn't seem to be too much fur that year. After debts had been paid, there was never a large surplus to be traded. Over the Christmas season, many of the Indians went down to Kenora or McIntosh to be with their children at the Indian Residential Schools.

My first Christmas and New Year's Day in Canada passed uneventfully at the post. There was no celebration, no Christmas tree and no special or, for that matter, different dinner. Donald got drunk on New Year's Eve.

Johnny Murchison came down from the outpost with the furs he had collected and did not return until the first week in January. He was short of some supplies, so our dog-team went along with him; Michell Keesik drove and I went along for the experience. As far as Johnny and Michell were concerned, I must have been just so much excess baggage and they didn't pay too much attention to me. The going was fairly good; they went ahead, trotting beside the dogs, and I followed as best I could.

At first I tried to keep up with them but found that this wasn't possible, so I just kept my own gait. Fortunately I had done a lot of cycling back home and my legs were in good shape so I managed to keep going without too much trouble. I caught up with them at lunch time. They had already eaten lunch, fed the dogs and were patiently waiting for me. As soon as I had gulped down my food, they repacked and set off again. I didn't catch up with them until we reached the outpost. It was a long day's trip, close to forty miles and I was very tired. I had made it all right though, and they grudgingly admitted that I could walk.

The return trip was much easier. We were going back empty and Michell allowed me to ride on the toboggan once in a while. As we went along, Michell pointed out a few wolf trails on the ice where bands of five or six wolves had crossed our path, but to my disappointment, we didn't see any. I had heard all of the wolf stories in my boyhood, but during my whole service with the Company I never came across any actual instance of wolves attacking travellers. There were many wolves in the area; the Ontario Provincial Government paid a bounty of $10.00 for each brush wolf or coyote and $25.00 for each timber wolf killed. They were usually caught in snares which were made of twenty strands of steel wire and were practically unbreakable. The trapper would bring the skin into the post where we made out a bounty application form. Then we sent the skin, with the form, to the Game and Fisheries Department in Toronto. We allowed the trapper to trade the amount of the bounty plus the value of the skin immediately. We kept the skin and the cheque when they came back from Toronto. The Game and Fisheries Department made two large, cross slashes in the mask of the wolf before returning it so that there was no chance of the same wolf being traded twice.

In deep snow, the Grassy Narrow Indians had a method of catching wolves which I have never seen anywhere else. They used especially long, narrow snowshoes — about six feet in length. Two or three of the Indians would set out on the hunt. When they came on a wolf track, they stepped up the pace, following the track until they caught sight of the wolf in the deep snow. Slowly but steadily, they edged it out onto a lake where they continued to chase it closely. Outnumbered, the wolf bounded through the drifts until it finally floundered in exhaustion. The hunters then dispatched it with a tap on the head with an axe.

*   *   *

During the winter, I made quite a few trips to the railroad with Michell and toward the end of the season he allowed me to drive the dogs, an experience I enjoyed very much. At last I was actually doing one of the things that I had dreamed of during the past winter. As I guided the dogs along the trail, I enjoyed the sight of plentiful wildlife: deer, bear and many different kinds of birds. I followed Michell's quietly spoken directions and made up my mind to ask him to teach me to handle a canoe the following summer. Although he was quiet and reserved, he was a good teacher and I learned much from watching him in all things and following his example.

At first I was amazed at how quickly he could get the fire going. He chose a suitable stopping place, grabbed his axe and disappeared into the bush while I unhitched the dogs so they could rest. We didn't have to chain them up but simply undid one of each dog's harness traces and they were able to lie down quite comfortably. Michell reappeared with a large green log of birch or poplar which he chopped in two and laid sideways on a bare spot. Then he brought a piece of dead tree — spruce or jackpine — and using the spruce twigs and birchbark as kindling, had a fire going in no time. The two green logs didn't burn immediately and were used to hold the large frying pan. Then he stuck two long sticks into the ground and on one hung the dog food pail and on

Dwelling house at Grassy Narrows, 1930. In the foreground, overturned, is a jumper sled for use on the lake ice in early spring.

Apprentice Ross with the Grassy Narrows dog team, at Long Legged Outpost, January 1931.

the other, our tea pail. The dog food, which was cornmeal and crackling, was cooked first and allowed to cool slightly before pouring a mess of it in front of each dog. In the meantime, I put a couple of cans of pork and beans with a few strips of salt pork into the frying pan and had it all sizzling. This, together with ship's biscuits, strawberry jam and strong, sweet tea, made a hearty and filling meal. In little over an hour, lunch was over; then we continued on to the station, picked up the mail and were on our way back to the post, arriving shortly after dark.

The first week in February, Michell made a special trip to the track and brought back John Patience, a fifth-year apprentice, who had been transferred from Dinorwic. I saw little of him; he spent the evening in the store with the boss and left early next morning to take charge of Long Legged Outpost from Johnny Murchison. I knew little or nothing of this arrangement, although I gathered from conversations in the store at Christmas time that the trappers were anything but happy with Johnny's management of the outpost. According to the March, 1931 issue of the Company's magazine *The Beaver*, J. R. Patience was transferred to Long Legged Outpost, replacing John Murchison 'who found it necessary to retire'. Johnny showed up at the post a few days later and left right away for the railway track. I never saw him again.

In late March, we were visited by J. W. Anderson, who was the inspector for the Superior-Huron District. He was later to become a legendary figure in the North, as district manager of the Eastern Arctic. Mr Anderson, or 'J.W.' as everyone in the Company later knew him, was an Aberdonian. His inspection was thorough.

He began by taking a physical inventory of all our stock in trade. I could see he wasn't too happy with it. There was a lot of old and unsaleable merchandise which was still being carried at regular inventory value. Most of this he wrote off and at one point, he sent me out to the lake with an ice chisel and instructions to dig a hole in the ice and dump in all the old ammunition we had been carrying for years. After the inventory had been taken and a profit percentage worked out, he checked all the books thoroughly; I was happy when he commended me on my bookkeeping. The last part of the inspection was his report which he typed out in triplicate before leaving the post. One copy was left on the post file after it had been discussed with the post manager and the original was forwarded by outgoing mail to District Office. The third copy was for Mr Anderson's own files.

Before leaving, Mr Anderson asked me how I was getting on. Realizing that I was hesitant to speak in front of Mr Murchison, he took me out for a long walk away from the post and talked to me like a Dutch uncle. I told him I was so fed up and so homesick that, if I had had the money, I would have returned to Scotland. After listening patiently, he pointed out that although things were bad, they were not all bad. I had mastered the bookkeeping, had a good knowledge of the Indian language and some insight into trading with Indians. In the end, he promised me a transfer to another post which would be more amenable, in the summertime. After he left, I felt more cheerful and began to look forward to my next posting, whenever and wherever it would be.

In accordance with Ontario Game and Fisheries regulations, the winter trapping season came to an end on March 10th and there was little doing by way of trade until the spring break-up, when the muskrat season opened. The days began to lengthen and the warmth of the sun could be felt. Crows put in their appearance from the south; this return of the little black crow, the Indians assured me, was a sure sign that spring was on its way.

As the snow disappeared, the lake became a sheet of glare ice. A jumper sleigh was used instead of a toboggan and the dogs could cover the ice at a tremendous speed. The only difficulty was on the portages, where the snow had melted. Any load had to be carried across on one's back; the dogs simply could not pull a loaded sleigh over the bare ground. The ice gradually began to candle and this constituted another problem. It was hard on the dogs' paws and they had to be fitted with deerskin moccasins. If the moccasins were tied on too tightly, they cut off the circulation and crippled the dogs; too loosely, they simply fell off.

By the end of April, creeks had opened up and were flowing freely. Where the river current passed through the lake, the ice disappeared rapidly. Soon the ice was candled so badly that it began to break up into huge chunks and swing around whenever the wind blew. This sight of my first spring break-up was an awesome one. The wind blew massive cakes of ice towards the island, smashing them up against the rocks where they broke up into small pieces and then melted in the warm sun.

With the arrival of open water, the Indians started muskrat trapping and there was a steady stream of customers coming into the store to trade in rat pelts. Mr Murchison had developed a system whereby he encouraged the natives who trapped locally to bring their skins in 'green' so that his wife and daughters had the job of putting them on stretchers to dry, thus earning themselves a little money. It was not unusual to have muskrat stretchers leaning against every wall in the house. Sometimes the Indians weren't too prompt in bringing their skins in and they had begun to stink. I couldn't see how the boss could grade the skins when they were brought into the store in this condition, but since he didn't encourage questions, I didn't ask.

The end of May was the official end of the Company's year. We took our annual inventory, made out all the year-end forms and forwarded them to District Office.

Then began the job of baling furs to be shipped to London, England. The fur press was hauled out from beneath the stairs, a length of hessian placed on the bottom and the furs carefully piled up until they came about two feet from the top. The rougher varieties, such as bearskins, were placed on the outside and the finer mink, silver or cross foxes, always in the centre. Then the top of the press was dropped down and a screw-jack inserted. This screw-jack enabled us to press the bale down to half its original size. Cross ropes were inserted through slots provided and securely lashed. Then the screw-jack was removed and the bale taken out. The edges of the hessian covering were sewn together with strong twine, each stitch knotted in such a way that if the twine should break or be cut, the rest would stay secure. Any knots or joins in this twine were sealed with brass seals bearing the Company's coat-of-arms. Both the heavy rope lashings and the twine used were of a special variety supplied by the Company for the sole purpose of fur baling. It was a combined twist of natural and red fibres.

All these precautions, Mr Murchison explained, were to prevent pilferage en route. The heavy screwing down was done to reduce the volume when the bales were shipped by steamer across the Atlantic; it also kept out pests which might get into the furs and damage them. When the bales were all ready, the last job was to stencil the London address of the Company on each side and to mark each end of the bale with the outfit, the initials HB, the post mark (K4 stood for Grassy Narrows), and the weight of the bale.

The May mail brought a letter from District Office that I was being transferred to Minaki, Ontario. I was to report there before the end of June. In the middle of June, I said goodbye to the Murchisons and to all my Indian friends, accompanied the mail canoe to Jones Station and caught the train west for Minaki.

I had been in Canada for almost one year.

3

MINAKI: SUMMER 1931

When I got off the train at Minaki, the first thing I saw was the post, situated on the side of a small incline about a hundred yards from the station, with a long wooden gangplank sidewalk leading up to it. I was to become very familiar with this gangplank in the days to come. I went into the store and introduced myself to the manager, Mr Louis Yelland. After a short conversation, he advised me that I would start work the following morning at 8 a.m. and then took me up to the house to meet his family.

Mrs Yelland was a cheerful, outgoing type and I liked her immediately. During the time I spent at Minaki, I never had any reason to change this opinion. She proved, moreover, to be an excellent cook. Gone were the austere meals of Grassy Narrows. We enjoyed all kinds of fresh vegetables and fruit and roasts of beef and pork. Two of their daughters, Jessie and Doreen, were at home when I arrived. Doreen was still a teenager and going to school. The other members of the family were three sons — Gordon, Jeff and Horace — and two daughters in Winnipeg. Jeff and Horace were attending St. John's College and came home for the summer when Horace shared my bedroom.

After supper, I went out to have a look around the settlement. The post was two storeys high, the main floor of which was the trading store. The walls were solid stone with two large plate glass display windows in front. The living quarters upstairs were of wooden frame construction with a living-room, dining-room, kitchen, bathroom and four bedrooms. Best of all, the building was equipped with running water and electric light supplied by the Canadian National Railway. While we had a bathtub and a

HBC Library

Store Manager Louis Yelland at Minaki. Merchandise was wheeled up wooden gangplanks to the warehouse and store from the railway station. 1920s.

HBC Library

In 1931 the Yelland family and H. M. Ross occupied the living quarters above the store. At left is the warehouse.

sink in the bathroom, there was no toilet. The outhouse, about fifty yards behind the building, was still the order of the day. There was a basement under the store with a room for storing coal and a large coal-burning furnace which heated the store and dwelling.

At one side of the store was a huge two-storey warehouse. The main floor was divided into a large general warehouse and a smaller flour warehouse. Upstairs, reached by a staircase from a separate door, were a number of bedrooms which were not in use. Behind the warehouse was a large ice-house.

The name 'Minaki' was the English for a descriptive Indian word meaning 'Beautiful Land' or 'Beautiful Place'. It wasn't old, compared with some of the Company's settlements on Hudson Bay or at Red River, but came into being when the railroad was first pushed west. The settlement was loosely spread over a large peninsula, jutting out between two big lakes, Sand Lake and Gunn Lake, forming part of the Winnipeg river system flowing north from Lake of the Woods. At the eastern end of the peninsula where the river narrowed, there was a spectacular steel railway bridge. There had been a large sawmill west of the station and the area was still referred to as 'the sawmill'. Although there were houses built on it, traces of the old sawdust dumps could be seen here and there. One part had been levelled out and a backstop built; it was here that I learned to play fastball.

A rough road went eastward from the station, past the inevitable water tower. About three hundred yards away, the road divided — one branch going north through the golf course to Minaki Lodge and the other east to Holst Point Lodge. Near the road junction was the provincial fire rangers' station. In the other direction, the road branched again — one route rambling north past the one-roomed schoolhouse to the lakeshore and the other going west towards the sawmill site.

Minaki Lodge was an imposing set of buildings of rough stone and logs. There was a large main house with an annex, and several separate cabins. It had its own power house for pumping water and generating electricity. Beside the power house was a boat-house where the lodge's launches and various small boats for angling were kept. There were four hard tennis courts and a

Western Canada Pictorial Index, CN Collection

Minaki Lodge, c. 1930.

beautiful nine-hole golf course, immaculately kept.

Holst Point was built completely of logs. In addition to the main lodge there were several small cabins and a small general store which was open during the summer season. Leonard Holst, the proprietor of Holst Point, was a middle-aged Scandinavian who was a great believer in physical exercise. He took great pride in his manly appearance and each morning, performed his exercises on the lawn in front of an admiring audience of female guests.

Minaki Lodge was geared to cater mainly to well-to-do Americans who came north for the fishing, while at Holst Point the clientele were mainly Canadians, the majority of them from Winnipeg. There always seemed to be a crowd of female school teachers there over the holidays.

Both the lakes were studded with islands of all sizes and shapes, and there were summer homes on almost all of them. There were also many summer cottages on the mainland on both sides of the river. Some belonged to Americans, but the majority were owned by people from Manitoba: grain merchants, doctors, or lawyers.

With the exception of a few families of railroad workers, the entire population of Minaki was geared towards the summer resort trade. They worked at either of the lodges, or for private cottagers as boatmen or guides, or on the golf course which had to be constantly maintained, as it had been laid down on solid rock.

There was no Indian reserve close by. The nearest was at White Dog roughly twenty miles north; another reserve was at One Man Lake, approximately sixty miles north of Minaki. Most of these Indians came down in the summer to a large encampment east of the river where they worked mainly as guides. In the autumn, they all disappeared north to their trapping grounds. We operated a trading post at One Man Lake.

Gunn Lake was reached from the station by a set of wooden steps and a wooden chute down which all baggage slid. There was a large dock for the convenience of the summer visitors. It was U-shaped and built about five feet above the water. This height was necessary because the water level fluctuated from summer to summer. The flow was regulated by a dam on the Winnipeg River at Kenora where the river flowed out from Lake of the Woods, and was subject to the requirements of the hydroelectric stations at the mouth of the Winnipeg River near Pine Falls.

At eight o'clock sharp, I presented myself for work. Mr Yelland was already there, standing at the door with his watch in his hand. This, I learned, was his regular procedure and woe betide me if I was late. I met the other regular employee at the store, Bob Scott, who had been hired as a storeman. He lived in the town and was a bachelor. Originally from Scotland, he had served overseas in World War I. He was a typical dour Scotsman but he gradually thawed out and we became fast friends. I owe a lot to him. He taught me everything about waiting on customers at the counter and never objected to answering my questions. He also taught me to speak Canadian. I learned to pronounce tomatoes to rhyme with potatoes; to ask for 12-gauge shells, instead of 12-bore cartridges, and found out that a 'Mac' was an apple and not a raincoat.

I might have been the 'gentleman' at Grassy Narrows but there was no fear of this happening at Minaki. It was work, work and then more work. My first job was to fill the iceboxes — one in the house, two big ones in the back shop — and the soft drink cooler. Bob patiently took me in hand: showed me how to clear away the sawdust insulation, slide out a large block using the ice tongs, and chop it into the required sizes with an ice-pick. Then the ice had to be washed and carried to its destination. After that, the grocery shelves had to be replenished from the reserve stock in the warehouse. The store was arranged in the same fashion as Grassy Narrows: groceries, drugs, tobacco and confectionary on one side, and dry goods and hardware on the other. There were the same type of counters, only there were racks with two different sizes of paper bags. The scales were much more up to date in that they showed the weight and the price of the article.

At one end of the counter was a bacon slicer, the cleaning of which was another of my daily jobs. Behind the counter stood a National Cash Register with two separate drawers. On this register I would ring up the individual items and then press the total button and get the amount of the sale which was recorded on tape inside the machine. No more drawers under the counter for cash. At the end of each day, the boss 'cashed up'. He counted out the $20.00 float, took the balance of the cash and tallied it up in the office. It had to balance exactly or there were questions asked.

At the rear of the store was the office which also served as a post office. Mr Yelland was the postmaster as well as the store manager. Mail came in daily on the 9 p.m. train. It was brought up to the post office, sorted and distributed to the waiting patrons before the day's work was finished. Outgoing mail was dispatched to Winnipeg each morning on the westbound train which stopped at Minaki at 5:30 a.m. As the junior member of the staff I was the one who had to get up at five in the morning to put the mail on the train.

The store didn't close for meals and we staggered our lunch and supper hours. I went to lunch at noon and was back in time to meet the 1:30 eastbound transcontinental train and bring up any fresh fruit or vegetables which had been ordered. After supper there was little to do until the eastbound train pulled in at nine. It brought the mail and our daily supply of bread and milk. In spring, there were only a few cases of each but as the season grew busy, the quantity increased to six or eight cases of bread and twenty cases of milk. But whether it was five cases or twenty, I hauled them all up the gangplank on a two-wheeled truck. Each milk case was solidly built of wood with a cover, and held twelve quarts of milk which had been packed in ice when shipped from Winnipeg. By the time the milk got to Minaki, most of the ice had melted. It was no easy job to lift these cases from the express car down to the truck. That water was icy cold and if I was not careful, I got drenched.

As soon as the mail sacks were delivered into the office, Mr Yelland closed the wicket and the office door and proceeded to sort the mail. It always seemed a strange coincidence that the wicket never opened again until the till had stopped ringing. When the mail had been picked up by the patrons and everyone had gone, the boss came out and told us to lock up. After the floors had been swept up and the lights turned out, Mr Yelland went slowly around the public areas of the whole store with a flashlight. He was, and rightly so, deathly afraid of fire and was always on the lookout for carelessly discarded cigarette butts.

This then was the daily routine, six days a week. I was firmly made to understand that I was not to go into the office unless invited in by the boss. He did the books and I was not allowed to touch them. My job was to serve behind the counter. Not until I had spent three summers at Minaki and was allowed a little more leeway, did I happen to find out, when I was asked to check through some old correspondence files, that the staff members were entitled to a half day off per week.

The freight came from Winnipeg once a week, usually late in the evening when the freight car was switched to a siding. Next morning, I would have the station master break the seals on the freight car door and give me the way-bills covering any freight consigned to the store. I didn't mind this part of the job too much except when we received the shipments of soft drinks, which came in large wooden cases containing four dozen bottles. These were heavy and awkward to handle. They had to be dragged across the floor of the railroad car to the door, lifted down, carried across the tracks to the platform, and then loaded onto my little truck and wheeled up past the store to the warehouse. There I stacked them ten cases high so that they used a minimum of floor space. If snow-shoes toughened my legs in the winter, the handling of soft drinks helped strengthen my upper body.

Only when we received a complete carload of flour, approximately forty tons, did Mr Yelland hire the services of the local
drayman, Roy Suffron. The flour came in the fall, coincidental
with the leaving of the supply brigade for One Man Lake Outpost.
The Indians manning the brigade helped us to load the sacks onto
the dray and then unload them into the warehouse. This operation always seemed to take place on a Sunday, my one day off. We
brought forward any flour still on hand in the warehouse, which
meant reversing the piles so that the top sacks would be on the
bottom. This removed any chance of the flour becoming hard-
packed and useless. Then we checked out the quantities going to
One Man Lake separately, took them down to the dock and
loaded them onto a waiting scow. It was a long day's work and as
far as Bob Scott and I were concerned, a day which we could have
cheerfully spent doing something else.

Mr Yelland was an Englishman and had served his time as a
draper in Manchester. He had always been on line posts, never
inland. Strict and methodical, he wanted everything done just so.
He spent all his time in the office and never waited on counter.
The only time he did any selling was during the trapping season.
When the Indians had traded in their furs in his office, it was our
job to sell them their grocery requirements. Then we advised Mr
Yelland how much they had spent for groceries. He then knew
how much cash each individual had left, came out behind the dry
goods counter and did his best to get back most of the money in
dry goods, which carried a much higher mark-up.

Mr Yelland was a great family man and seldom left the post.
He owned a boat and outboard motor and occasionally he
allowed one of his boys to take him out for a spin on the lake. He
suffered greatly from severe headaches which lasted for days at a
time and consumed a tremendous number of 292s, a very strong
aspirin tablet.

He was, moreover, an excessive cigar smoker but fussy about
the brand he smoked. Woe betide the poor salesman who ventured into his office to display his wares or to take an order
without first buying Mr Yelland a couple of 'House of Lords'
cigars at the counter and presenting them to him. No matter what
product he represented, he didn't get an order unless the cigars
were forthcoming.

The stocks in the store were quite similar to those carried at Grassy Narrows but in greater variety, due to the more sophisticated tastes of the vacationers. Indians liked what they liked and weren't too adventurous in their selection of store-bought foods. A quart of milk or a loaf of bread sold for 9¢ and two cans of peas, corn or tomatoes went for 25¢. There was no liquor store nearer than Kenora but we were permitted to carry a type of light beer which was almost non-alcoholic. We sold lots of it, especially to the Indians.

While artificial extracts used for baking were openly displayed on the shelves, pure extracts had to be kept under the counter, as they contained a high percentage of alcohol. The Indians were constantly pleading with us to sell them 'just one bottle' to mix with the beer to give it a kick. Naturally, we refused to do this; it was against the law, and the Company's regulations, to sell intoxicants to Indians. The fine could be high if one were caught.

One of the boss's procedures surprised me. Many of our local customers had run up unpaid bills in the past and were barred from further credit. It they were able to land a temporary job, however, they came into the office and had a chat with Mr Yelland who would then sell them anything they required and 'just put it in the little black book'. The little black book was a version of what I later came to know as the vest-pocket ledger. It was kept behind the cash register. Such transactions were duly recorded and when paid for, were rung up in the till as cash sales.

Some of the summer residents were already occupying their cottages but the big influx didn't start until July 1st after schools had closed in Winnipeg. During these June weeks, I got to know some of the local people.

Bert Cleavely was the local chief fire ranger. The crew consisted of Sid Turner, deputy chief; Ab Dusang, who drove the launch; Ab's two sons, Reg and Gerald; Peter Black, the cook; and Eddie Anderson, whose main job seemed to be keeping the grounds tidy and recruiting native labour whenever a fire broke out. There were fire towers at various points in the area, manned with rangers watching for any trace of smoke. When fires were reported to Minaki, they were triangulated on a map and the

Mrs. H. G. McKenty, cottage owner at Minaki, with H. M. Ross in the Hudson's Bay Minaki store. 1931.

The interior of the Minaki store, displaying groceries and fresh produce.

exact position determined. If the fire was near the shore of any of the main lakes, the fire fighters were ferried out in their own launch. But if the fire was inland, a forestry plane from Kenora was called into use to fly the fire fighters to the spot. They were completely equipped with gasoline-driven water pumps, lengths of hose and an ungainly apparatus called a water-jack. This was a type of packsack which held about ten gallons of water, with a hose and nozzle attached. It weighed about a hundred pounds and was awkward to handle. When the fire had been nearly extinguished, the fire rangers patrolled the perimeters carrying these water-jacks on their backs, quickly putting out any little outbreak or smoldering patch.

The chief ranger had the power to co-opt any male to go fire-fighting. They were paid a reasonable wage, their board, tobacco, and compensation for any clothing that was scorched or damaged during the fire. We were always busy in the store when a fire was reported. Large orders of groceries — bacon, beans, tea, flour, sugar, coffee and tobacco — had to be put up immediately. I got to know the deputy chief and Mrs Turner well; their son Dick became my closest friend during my stay at Minaki.

Dick Giroux had his dock and gas station at one end of the government dock. He had the main delivery service by boat and looked after a few privately owned camps. In the winter months, he put up their wood and ice.

Across the bay was Roy Grellier's boat house. As well as running this, Roy was an expert marine mechanic and attended to all repairs and servicing of boats and motors, both inboard and outboard, for which he also had an agency. Madame Grellier was a Parisian by birth, just over five feet tall, with a large aristocratic nose. I always described her in my mind as *très formidable*. She was not too fluent in English, and, in the beginning, a bit reserved in the store. When I tried my schoolboy French on her she brightened up considerably, and from then on we spoke in both languages to help each other. She was a marvelous cook but her specialty was her coffee. Whenever I visited the house, there was always a brew of good strong coffee on the stove.

Art Spillet was the local game warden, and each summer

there was a representative of the Ontario Provincial Police in residence.

Jim Hayward, an Englishman, had a house about half a mile from town. He owned his own boat and did a lot of work as a fishing guide. A former sailor in the British Navy, Jim showed me — when hoisting the Company's flag daily — how to fold it properly, put a loop around it and break it out at the masthead. As a former sailor, he also added considerably to my vocabulary.

The station agent was John Charlton, whose son Roy was the telegraph operator. Charlton had a disability in one hand, but he was still one of the best shotgun handlers that I have ever met. Few ducks got by him.

Hughie Weir was employed as a carpenter at Minaki Lodge. He had served his apprenticeship as a cabinet maker in the Old Country, and his workmanship was something to behold. His wife came from Archiestown, just a few miles from my hometown, so naturally we spent much time discussing mutual friends and comparing the beauty of Speyside to Minaki.

Like clockwork, every Friday two old codgers came into the store. They lived about two miles west of the settlement and walked in for their mail and supplies. Both were old age pensioners, as erect and spry as anyone twenty years their junior. Henry Greenslade was a health addict and fifty years ahead of his time. He looked as if he lived on Roman meal, Lishus, and Brekus Puddy, health foods that were much in vogue at the time.

The other oldtimer, Bill McMasters, was an Irishman with a keen sense of humour. He and I got along splendidly. While I always called Mr Greenslade by his proper name, it wasn't long before I was calling Mr McMasters 'Bill'. It was rumoured around town that he had originally come out to Canada as the 'black sheep' of a landed Irish family, but whether it was true or not I don't know.

I gradually got to know a group of young fellows all about my own age. They were a great bunch and we had many good times together, although they sometimes laughed at my Scottish expressions. There was Dick Turner; Jim and Herb Hayward; Aldyn Stone; Bobby Babineau, the section foreman's son; Roy

McNally, who lived with his widowed mother and younger brother; and Bert Weir. Together they decided to make me a real Canadian, and began by introducing me to the game of baseball. Since it resembled 'rounders', a ball game played by schoolgirls in Britain, I soon picked up the rules. When I told them I had played a bit of cricket and usually was wicketkeeper, I was promptly appointed catcher.

George and Art Jenkins lived at the old sawmill with their widowed father. George played the cello and Art, the violin. Both were accomplished musicians and after the summer was over, we had many musical evenings at Sid Turner's house. Dick played the banjo well and Sid was a fine pianist.

Naturally enough, there were also a number of young ladies: Dorothy Suffron; Disa Stone; Pearl, Frankie and Opal Giroux; Peggy Turner, Dick's young sister; and Iris Paterson. While I secretly admired the open, friendly manner in which I was made part of the group, I didn't pay too much attention to the girls. I was busy in the store, but more importantly, there was Peggy Miller, the girl I had become engaged to in Scotland before coming to Canada. I thought myself to be very much in love and spent many evenings writing to her.

But it wasn't a case of all work and no play. At the end of June, the staff for both Minaki Lodge and Holst Point arrived. They were mostly university students from Winnipeg who worked as waitresses or bellhops. There were staff dances on the top floor of the Lodge's boat-house every week and hops at Holst Point almost every night, especially when we could get someone to play the piano there. I was really enjoying myself for the first time since I had arrived in Canada. But there were quite a few mornings when it was all I could do to get myself out of bed to put the mail on that 5:30 a.m. train.

We could buy a gallon jug of wine — either white Branvin or a red Catawba — from the liquor store in Kenora for $2.00. Bill Letwinuk, who occasionally worked on the section and cut hair in his spare time, sold a good brand of home-brew to privileged customers at 25¢ for a pop bottle full. If we drank it straight, it would knock our socks off, but mixed with a bottle of Kia-Ora lemon squash, it made a very palatable drink indeed. If we were in funds or had a particularly heavy date, Mah Jong, the laundry-man at Holst Point, could always supply a bottle of good liquor at a reasonable price. I'm sure the local representative of the Ontario Provincial Police had an inkling of what was going on, but provided that we were discreet, he didn't bother us. Every once in a while, Bill Letwinuk was hauled up before Mr Charlton, who doubled as the local magistrate, for bootlegging. It usually ended up with Bill being fined $5.00 and promising to mend his ways. Sometimes though, Mr Charlton would reach into his own pocket to pay the fine until such time as Bill could pay him back.

My first summer season at Minaki was hectic but I survived. By Labour Day, most of the visitors had returned home and the lodges started to close up. Then the settlement reverted to its winter peace and quiet.

After we had sent the freight brigade safely on its way to One Man Lake, things slowed down in the store. We closed up shop at six o'clock, but opened again at nine for the handling of the mail, milk and bread.

In mid-September, instructions came from District Office that I was to proceed to Grassy Narrows once again to run Long Legged Outpost for the coming winter. I was not sorry to leave Minaki. I had enjoyed the posting but, after all, it was only a store clerking job. I preferred to be back in the bush, handling furs and trading with my Indian friends.

On the appointed day, I boarded the train for Jones Station to catch the mail canoe for Grassy Narrows.

4

LONG LEGGED OUTPOST: WINTER 1931-32

What a change I found at Grassy Narrows. Donald Murchison had retired at the end of June and gone with all his family to Gull Bay on Lake Nipigon. John Patience, who had run Long Legged Outpost, was now in charge. He had come out from Avoch in Rosshire and, his apprenticeship completed, was in charge of his first post.

He told me that a new dwelling had been built at Long Legged Outpost but it was not completely finished. I had to leave as soon as possible to put the finishing touches to the house before the winter set in. In a few days, we had my wintering outfit together and the freighters left with two loaded canoes. I went along in the small canoe with my old friend Michell Keesik. He was to stay with me to help finish the house and then would return with the canoe to Grassy Narrows.

The trip took us only three days; there was just one intervening portage — a small carry-over at Maynard Falls. The weather was fine and the countryside in the full blaze of autumn. I had become quite proficient with the paddle during the summer but hadn't made any long trips. Paddling around in a canoe on a Sunday afternoon is one thing, but slugging it out, mile after mile for a whole day, is another thing entirely. I developed a hotbox behind my left shoulder and by noon the first day, I was in agony. On top of this, I wasn't sitting on the seat of the canoe but had to kneel, Indian fashion. Usually we paddled for an hour, rested for ten minutes and had a smoke. Eventually, I was able to ignore the soreness in my shoulder and knees and enjoy the trip.

One night we went moose hunting in a deep bay which was

Long Legged Outpost. Winter 1931.

covered with water lilies. This was my first moose hunt. We camped on an island and after supper, just before dusk, the Indians paddled over into the bay and we took up our positions on shore.

John Loon, one of the freighters, made a birch-bark horn which he took with him. He also carried a kettle full of water. Not knowing what on earth he was going to do with a kettle of water and the birch-bark horn, I stayed close by him and watched. He put the horn to his mouth and blew into it, producing the most horrible noises. It sounded much like a cow in pain — but it was effective. Soon we heard a thrashing in the bushes, but no moose appeared. Slowly John raised the kettle of water to his shoulder. Then he poured it out on the ground in a steady, noisy stream. That did the trick. Instantly, a huge bull moose appeared, thrashing heavily along the shore among the lily pads. I think every Indian in the party must have shot at it at the same time, for it crashed to the ground immediately. I sure was glad that the Indians were there with their 30.30 carbines, because my little .22 rifle wouldn't have been of much use against such a tremendous beast. Anyway, I was shaking so much with excitement that I doubt if I could have pulled the trigger. In a short time, the moose was gralloched, skinned and cut up into pieces. We were soon back at camp where we had a grand meal and stuffed ourselves with moose meat.

At the outpost, the crew didn't waste any time. They quickly unloaded the freight into the small warehouse and were on their way back to Grassy Narrows. They were in a hurry to get away to their traplines.

Long Legged Outpost was a lonely spot, miles from anywhere. There was a trading store, a warehouse, the old dwelling house and a brand new cabin which had been built on the slope beside two towering pine trees. There were a few native shacks around, which the trappers used on the way to and from the trapping grounds. The outpost itself was situated on a promontory at the east end of Oak Lake where the Long Legged River joined the English River in a series of waterfalls.

The first priority was to get the cabin weatherproofed for the winter. It was well constructed of peeled logs and a pole roof. A sufficient supply of lumber had been brought along. Michell and I laid a roof over the pole rafters. On top of this we applied heavy tarpaper. It wasn't a difficult job. The rolls of tarpaper were put across the roof, nailed down with flat-headed nails and, where there was an overlap, firmly sealed down with liquid tar, cans of which were supplied with each roll of roofing.

Next we laid the floor and then inserted the door and two small windows in the openings which had been previously cut. The inside walls were lined with a heavy grade building paper, put on vertically, slightly overlapping in the same manner as the roof.

The openings between the logs in the walls were packed as tightly as possible with dried moss, and then shingle nails were knocked in along these openings about six inches apart. This gave a hold for the mud that we applied next. After searching around, we found a suitable deposit of clay soil. We puddled it with warm water to make a firm plaster and laced it liberally with chopped hay to act as a binding. We applied this mixture over the moss between the logs with our bare hands.

We carried the cast-iron cookstove up from the old dwelling and set it in a corner, back to back with an airtight heater. Although the cookstove was old, it was still in good condition, had an oven which worked and four lids on top for cooking. The heater was an oval tin stove with a lining at the bottom and two dampers. Its chief advantage was that it threw a strong heat quickly, but steady control of the dampers was required so that it didn't overheat and turn cherry red. We hooked the two stoves together by elbows to one stove-pipe which ran through a roof jack in the roof.

That evening I told Michell that I wouldn't require his services any longer and that he could leave the next morning. But when morning dawned, poor Michell was suffering from a bad stomach-ache and he refused to get out of bed. He just lay there and in usual stoical Indian fashion, said that he would go the next day if he was better. I was worried about him but he said it was simply a case of 'he would get better or he would die.' I was greatly relieved when he started to show improvement by late evening and the following day he was well enough to be on his way.

When I saw him disappear down the path it was a great moment for me. I was nineteen years old and for the first time, completely on my own in the wilds of Canada. This was what I dreamed it would be like when I first thought of leaving Scotland. Well, I wasn't completely alone. In his desire to cut down on post expenses, John Patience had decided to do away with the dog-team. He planned to hire a local team whenever the need arose. So I had asked to keep the lead dog, Caesar, a black and white collie. He was a most intelligent animal and we became inseparable companions. In the days that followed, we explored every trail around the outpost.

The cabin measured about 20 by 24 feet, and other than the two stoves, there wasn't a stick of furniture in it. I spent the first day cutting branches from small balsam trees and weaving them into a fine thick mattress; this I put into a corner and covered it with a tarpaulin, flannelette sheets and my pair of Hudson's Bay blankets. I made a pillow by stuffing an old flour sack with balsam needles. The aroma was a bit overpowering at first but it certainly cleared the nostrils.

The top of a wooden packing crate made a serviceable table after I covered it with a yard of oilcloth. It was hinged against the wall under the window and propped up with a stick when it was required. I used a large block of firewood for a chair — primitive but adequate. I found an empty biscuit barrel in the store and from it I fashioned a simple armchair and stuffed a flour sack with hay for a cushion. This was my first attempt at constructing furniture. It took considerable ingenuity and a lot of common sense, but the end justified my labour. A piece of lumber did for a shelf to hold my books, and I put a large Hudson's Bay calendar on one wall and the coal-oil lamp on another. As I had eight gallons of coal-oil to last the entire winter, it had to be rationed out carefully. Going to bed soon after dark and getting up at sunrise became a necessary routine.

As always, there was little firewood cut, so I knocked down the old log dwelling, sawed it up into logs, split them and piled them beside the door. This dried wood was fine for the cookstove but I needed green birch for the heater. Each day, Caesar and I went exploring our surroundings. I always took an axe with me and whenever I spied suitable birch, I chopped it down and cut it into carrying lengths. Whenever I had a spare moment around the post I got the bucksaw out and sawed the birch trees into stove lengths. In this way, I accumulated a sufficient supply of wood for the coming winter.

After getting the house straightened away, my next job was to unpack, check and display my merchandise in the trading store. We only carried the essentials at the outpost, and this work didn't take too long. As the days grew colder, I noticed that a plague of field mice had moved into the store and warehouse. For about a week, I was busy taking precautions against mouse damage. All the flour had to be piled up on a raised platform and the legs of it lined with tin, which stuck out in such a fashion that the rodents couldn't climb out over it to get at the flour. Similarly, six-pound bags of rolled oats were hung from nails knocked into the rafters. The sacks dangled from quite long ropes which passed through inverted tin plates, again baffling the mice. I had a few mousetraps but they couldn't cope with the numbers, so I rigged up my own trap. Using a large ten-gallon pail, half filled with water, I laid narrow pieces of board against it. Then I dangled a juicy piece of salt pork from a nail, directly over the pail. When the mice smelled the pork, they ran up the boards to get at it, and overbalancing, fell into the water and drowned. Soon the invasion was brought under control.

John Patience had increased the varieties of groceries considerably at Grassy Narrows, so my mess supplies included several different kinds of canned fruits, a couple of cases of Carnation milk and a few cases of canned sausages and corned beef. I didn't starve. In fact, with the partridge and prairie chicken I was able to bag with my shotgun, I lived quite high on the hog. On one occasion, I even had fresh meat in my larder. Looking out the window one afternoon, I spotted a deer browsing among the poplar trees a couple of hundred yards away. I got my rifle, locked the dog in the house and proceeded cautiously to stalk the deer. I downed it with one shot and Caesar and I gorged ourselves for several days on the venison.

There was lots of time to improve my cooking skills. By experimenting, I was able, finally, to produce a superior type of bannock much like the scones my mother used to bake. A little dried milk, some raisins and less lard did the trick. After a few failures, which even Caesar turned his nose up at, I was able to make pastry and thereafter, I regularly baked pies filled with raisins or dried apples or both. I used a lot more rice and stayed away from the dried navy beans.

Laundry was done once a week. True, I didn't iron my shirts, but they were at least clean. In preparation of my going to Canada, my mother had taught me to darn socks, sew on buttons and make a decent patch. Every Sunday, I made it a point to have a thorough wash, shave and hair trim. Then I donned a white shirt and wore my oxfords instead of the moccasins which were my daily footwear. This was a practice I followed during the time I 'bached' it in the bush. It was not uncommon for men alone in the North to let themselves go. My routine was, I suppose, a safeguard against getting 'bushed', as it was called.

All in all, the days passed quickly and I wasn't lonely. Towards the end of October canoes began to appear on the lake — trappers on their way north. Some of them just said 'hello' in passing, but others would stop for a night or two and trade for any articles they had forgotten to buy at the main post. If there was any mail, they brought it to me. I got lots of bundles of magazines from my chums at Minaki and didn't go short of reading material.

When I had been advised at Minaki that I was being posted to Long Legged Outpost, I had placed an order with our Winnipeg Supply Depot and one day my purchases showed up — a spring-wind portable gramophone, a dozen records and a banjolele. The banjolele is smaller than a banjo and the fingering is the same as for the violin. One simply plucked the strings instead of drawing a bow over them. As a booklet of instructions was enclosed, I spent my evenings mastering it and eventually, could pick out simple tunes. I thought it sounded rather good. Caesar hid in the corner whenever I took the instrument off the wall.

It wasn't long before freeze-up came again. I was marooned until the ice became thick enough for winter travelling. After a few weeks, trappers began drifting down from the north. They only brought sufficient furs with them to cover the price of the necessities they were short of. Usually they arrived in the evening and slept in my house. Before trading, they had a meal of a half can of beans per man, four ship's biscuits, some lard, jam and all the tea they could drink. It was considered polite by the Indians to eat everything that was placed in front of them, hence the rationing. Once the meal was finished we proceeded with the trading. If there was any credit balance left, the trapper was given a credit note which was redeemable either at the outpost or at Grassy Narrows. With business concluded, the trappers lay down on the floor to sleep.

Each had a deerskin with the hair left on, which they used as a mattress, and a rabbitskin robe. There were no such things as sleeping bags in those days, but a well made rabbitskin robe was hard to beat. It was light, comfortable and warm, even in the coldest temperatures. Green rabbitskins were cut in a spiral in one continuous piece and then twisted around like a rope. Then they were hung outside to dry. The next step was to weave these strings like a carpet. When this was done properly, it was practically impossible to find any holes in the completed article. Then it was placed inside a double flannelette blanket, the edges sewn up and stitched in the centre like a quilt.

Next morning the Indians would be up bright and early, pack their toboggans and be on their way back to the trapping grounds by the time the sun was over the horizon.

Around the 18th of December, they drifted back to spend Christmas at Grassy Narrows or down at the track with their children. For a week or so, I was extremely busy at the store until they had all gone south. It had been arranged that I would go down to Grassy to spend Christmas and New Year's with John Patience. In preparation for this, I made a harness for Caesar and repaired an old hand toboggan that I had found in the warehouse. Lashing my pack of fur and my grub box on the sleigh and sticking in my hatchet, I set out early in the morning. With all the travel over it, the trail was granite hard and the dog was able to pull the toboggan easily so we made good time. It was a beautiful day with no wind, but very cold. So cold, in fact, that I was glad I was wearing a black silk kerchief, a trick I had learned from the Indians. It was light enough to allow me to breathe through it, and eliminated any danger of freezing my lungs. It was a long day's walk and I was fairly tuckered out when I finally reached the post.

John Patience was glad to see me and we sat up talking late into the night. He was suffering badly from toothache and was living on aspirin. He had written for and received permission to proceed to Winnipeg for dental treatment. I was to stay and look after the post until his return.

I felt sorry for John. This was his first post and he was strictly following instructions to cut down on his expenses. His supply of wood for the winter was inadequate. He would put only one log at a time into the stove in the house. When it began to get cold, he put on a sweater, then another, then draped a blanket over his shoulder, before he would grudgingly place another log on the fire. His favourite dish was what he called, in his broad Scottish accent, 'Welsh Rabbit' — ship's biscuits heated in the frypan along with cheese which melted over them. He was quite upset over the fact that he had saved so much on his mess budget the previous year that the Company had cut down his current allowance by $5.00 a month. I'm afraid I didn't express too much sympathy for him; I thought it was mainly his own fault.

Trade was brisk in the store just before Christmas and it was not until all the customers had been looked after and their accounts settled up, that John left for Winnipeg. He returned ten days later feeling much more cheerful after his visit to the bright lights and with his dental problems attended to. Next day, I returned to my outpost, accompanied by Michell Keesik and a dog-team load of supplies.

The balance of the winter passed smoothly, with no major problems. In time, I became more confident in my fur buying and I spent a lot of time grading and regrading the fur which I had already purchased. It was a case of reading and re-reading the fur purchasing manual and checking with my fur tariff, so that I could set a proper standard for myself. Buying good fur was never difficult. Low grade, late or damaged skins were more difficult. My method was to set what I thought was a fair price for such a skin and not to budge from it. I would sooner lose a poor skin than overpay for it and thus reduce any profit that would be made on the good skins. Mostly, the trappers accepted my valuations and seemed to think that I knew what I was doing.

Late in March, I had a visit from the district inspector. He had been at Grassy Narrows and decided at the last minute to come up to my outpost. Matt Cowan was a tall, unmarried Scot from Edinburgh; he had replaced J. W. Anderson, who had taken over the management of James Bay the previous year. He arrived late in the evening with Michell and after a meal, made a cursory examination of the store and warehouse. We spent the evening talking and he left again first thing in the morning. Although he told me that I would be returning to Minaki for the coming summer season, I was puzzled by his visit. Later on, I found out that he had visited all outposts in the district that winter to decide whether any or all of them should be closed. Long Legged Outpost was not operated the following winter.

After the spring break-up, when the Indians had finished their muskrat hunting, Michell paddled up to get me. We closed up the buildings and packed up the remains of the stock to be taken back with us to Grassy. There, I helped John Patience to bale fur and, at the end of May, left once more for Minaki.

5

MINAKI: 1932-33

My first assignment at Minaki was to go to One Man Lake Outpost to take an inspection inventory. As a guide Mr Yelland had hired Tom Young, who had retired from the Company's service some years earlier. He had been in charge of White Dog Outpost, which was now closed down, and he lived with his wife on an island across the bay from Minaki. We set off bright and early by canoe. At first I was troubled by the old hotbox on my shoulder, but by the time we reached the falls at White Dog, I was in good shape.

The White Dog Falls consisted of one sheer drop and two separate series of rapids. They were very beautiful and we had to make a portage around each of them. Unfortunately, the falls are gone now, since a hydroelectric dam was built there in the 1950s. Tom told me that in the old days, there had been a light railway on the other side of the river which circumvented the falls and had been used for hauling York boats across. If we had had more time, we would have examined the site of this old York boat railway.

Below the falls, we entered a quiet stretch of the river, both sides of which were lined with wild plum trees in full blossom. Red-winged blackbirds loudly proclaimed their territories from the reeds along the banks, and large black crows called an alarm as we silently paddled down the quiet stream. Soon we entered the mouth of the White Dog River and paddled up to the old Hudson's Bay buildings, which were situated at the edge of the White Dog Indian Reserve. The river meanders through a grassy valley lined with Indian houses on either side; it is one of the most picturesque reservations I have ever seen. We had the keys to the abandoned buildings and spent the night there. The old house was still in fairly good condition. The outside was plastered in a different manner than usual: long withes had been nailed diagonally across the logs and the whole thing plastered smoothly and then whitewashed. Inside, the rooms were lined with tongue-and-groove lumber halfway up the walls, and the upper half, finished with hessian. It was very effective.

Upstairs in the store all the old post records were laid out on a long table; its legs had been fitted half-way up with tin plates to keep off mice. All the entries were in beautiful copperplate writing. Tom told me that they were the handiwork of S. A. Taylor, who had been manager at White Dog for many years. In one corner, there were a number of old muzzle-loading muskets. I wish now that I had helped myself to one.

Next morning we locked up the buildings and paddled up the White Dog River. From it, we portaged over to Goshawk Lake and then, finally, into One Man Lake. It was a long paddle across the lake before we finally reached the outpost.

One Man Lake Outpost was built on the northeast end of the lake into which the English River flows. The buildings were about a quarter of a mile from the boundary of the reserve which stretched all along the northern shore of the lake. The post buildings were built of logs. The house had one very large room and a stairway leading up to a floored attic.

Battiste Fisher, the manager, had been advised of my coming and was prepared. He was an Ojibway, drawing near to retirement age. He had already built a house on the reserve for his wife and himself and their two grown-up sons. There he would live comfortably on his pension.

There was little inventory to take, as Battiste had run the stocks low. His furs were already baled, so one day's work completed everything and we took off for Minaki. But this time we didn't paddle. Battiste owned a large, square-sterned canoe with an Elto outboard motor. It had no starting cord but a large flywheel on top, with a knob attached. He grabbed the knob, spun the flywheel frantically and away we went, towing the large freight canoe loaded with the bales of fur and our canoe tied across the top. Battiste's sons accompanied us to do the necessary

Portaging from White Dog River to Goshawk Lake,
1933.

White Dog Falls, 1933.

portaging. Two days later we arrived at Minaki. The summer passed in the usual manner with lots of hard work and plenty of hard play.

At a dance at Holst Point, I met a girl from Winnipeg, a Miss Beatrice Dingle, who liked to play tennis. As I had played before, we made up a game and it soon became a regular habit. Horace, the boss's son, who shared my room when he was home, was a good head and we became friends. When his girl friend came down from Winnipeg, the four of us decided to go to the Saturday night dance at Minaki Lodge. This was a formal affair with an orchestra from Winnipeg to play for us. The ladies wore long dresses, and white flannels and blue blazers were the required dress for gentlemen. Since I didn't own either, Horace wired my measurements to his brother Jeff in the city and when the clothes arrived, I attached my Elgin Academy Former Pupils Association badge to the blazer. We had such a good time at the dance that we decided to make our foursome a regular outing.

But it was quite a chore to keep those white flannels clean. We solved the problem by dipping them in high test gasoline and hanging them on the washline for a couple of days to blow away the smell. And we had to be very careful with lit cigarettes.

In the middle of September, Mr Yelland called me into his office. 'Do you know a James Holden?' he asked.

'Yes, I do,' I replied. 'He came out with me in 1930. I think he's from Campbelltown in Argyll-shire.'

'That's fine. I've just received a letter from District Office. You are to catch the eastbound train tomorrow afternoon and meet Mr Holden on the train. He'll have further information for you. That's all the letter says, except that you'll be gone for about two weeks.'

Perplexed, I boarded the train the next day and there was Jimmy Holden, looking for me. 'What's this all about, Jimmy? It sounds very mysterious.'

He handed me the letter. 'That's our letter of instructions. Read it for yourself.' The letter baldly said that we were to get off the train at Armstrong, a divisional point, and there catch the weekly local to Cavell Post. When we got there, Jimmy was to take charge of the post and we were to see that the present post

The Hudson's Bay Company store at Cavell, Ontario, 1933.

manager, Johnny Goodwin, and his wife were off the premises as soon as possible. After we had done this, we had to take an inventory. Then Jimmy was to accompany the outpost manager with the freight brigade to Nazatekang Outpost and open it up for the winter. I was to return to Minaki. Neither Jimmy nor I knew what to expect when we arrived at Cavell. Fortunately, the job wasn't too unpleasant. Johnny Goodwin was ready for us. He had packed all his belongings and pitched a tent by the side of the railway. After we checked the cash and he had handed over the keys to the buildings, he got off the Company's property immediately and camped beside the tracks until the westbound local arrived.

  Johnny's problem was liquor. When the thirst was on him, he locked up the store and walked the tracks to Nakina, a divisional point about eleven miles east where there was a beer parlour. Unfortunately, once he began to drink, he didn't know when to stop and it might be several days before he returned to the post. His other mistake was that he just stuffed a handful of money in his pocket from the till without charging it up to himself. When he returned, he would balance the cash and whatever amount was missing he figured he had spent on drink and then charged it up to his own account. This had been going on for quite a while and might have continued, except that the Company inspector called in at the post unexpectedly, when Johnny was away. Now he was on his way to an early retirement.

We took a merchandise inventory and balanced the books. While doing the inventory, we discovered that chipmunks had made nests and were breeding behind bolts of dry goods on the shelves. Jimmy and I took a .22 rifle each from stock and settled ourselves quietly on the opposite counter. Whenever a chipmunk showed its face, we fired. It was messy but necessary, and we took no great pleasure in it. Without this action, a large quantity of valuable merchandise would have been ruined. In this one afternoon, we cleared them all out.

There was a large amount of cash and cheques on hand so a remittance had to be sent to District Office right away. The local train only ran once a week, so it was decided that one of us would walk to Nakina which had the nearest post office. We tossed a coin and I lost. So the following day, in the rain, I walked the track to the post office, eleven miles there and eleven miles back. On my return, I gave Jimmy such a glowing description of the female clerks in the post office that he vowed that he would make the next trip and I could man the post. Cavell was a small settlement. There had once been a sawmill but it had ceased operations. The few people, both Indian and half-breed, who had worked at the mill, still lived around and traded at the post.

The following week, Jimmy left with the native outpost manager and the freight brigade to set up and inspect the wintering outpost at Nazatekang. There wasn't much doing in the store; most of my evenings were spent at a beautiful little river I discovered behind the property. It was full of square-tailed trout, with a deep pink flesh. It was marvellous to be able to drop a line into any stream and fish without looking over my shoulder for a water bailiff. In Scotland, all the water is privately owned and although you could take a trout, any salmon had to be either thrown back or given to the laird. Unless, of course, you were as good a poacher as my father.

When Jimmy returned, I caught the train back to Minaki,

where I learned I was to stay for the winter. I would have preferred to go back into the bush but orders were orders. In the fall, we had corn roasts, weiner roasts and bonfire parties by the lake and occasionally, midnight swimming parties.

Most of the local people had European backgrounds and were familiar with the game of soccer. To my surprise, I found that Mr Yelland had been an ardent soccer player. He played goalkeeper in his youth and was still a strong supporter of Manchester United. He agreed to act as referee for us, and every Sunday afternoon we had a rough and tumble game on a flat meadow across the river from Holst Point.

When the hunting season opened, we wandered over the golf course in the evenings, shooting prairie chickens. Mrs Yelland had only one stipulation — they had to be plucked and cleaned when we brought them home. I had a little .410 single shot shotgun but I was a poor shot. In fact, I never did master the use of the shotgun and it was seldom that I had any chickens to pluck and dress.

I felt sorry for the local men. Their work was strictly seasonal and if they had not made enough during the summer months to tide them over the winter, their situation could be grim. They went into the bush to cut cordwood. It was hard work; there were no chainsaws then. They walked a long way into the bush, spent the time cutting and stacking wood and then walked back home. The wood sold for $2.00 a cord — slim pickings indeed. Once the ice was deeply frozen, the only other work available was the cutting up and storing of ice at both the lodges and the various summer homes.

With the soccer season over, we spent our Sunday afternoons playing hockey. A space between the docks was cleared off and we made it into a skating rink. I had never played the game and, for that matter, had never even been on skates before. I was game for anything so I swapped my violin for a pair of second-hand skates and was soon staggering around on the ice. I spent so much time on my backside that it was unanimously decided that I should play in goal, where I could hang onto the goal posts. We had no sophisticated equipment — none of us could afford it — so we improvised. Hockey sticks were made from curved birch branches; and Eaton's catalogues, stuffed down our stockings, made good padding.

Friday night was dance night during the winter months. There was another store building about 200 yards away from the Bay store that was used as an ice-cream parlour during the summer but closed up shop once the tourists had gone home. Its main advantage was that it held a piano, so we arranged to have the use of the building for the dances. There were two types of dancing — regular ballroom and square dancing. In Scotland, I had learned to do the eightsome reel, the lancers, and the quadrilles, but square dancing was different. I had to pay close attention to the caller as he chanted out the figures he wanted performed. By watching the other dancers and listening carefully, I soon was do-si-doing with the rest. This was not formal stuff. The music was fast and furious and the object seemed to be to try to swing your partner off her feet. There were no cliques. We tried to dance with every woman present whether she was a girl of thirteen or a matron of sixty.

Music was provided by Sid Turner at the piano, Dick Turner on his banjo, George Jenkins on the cello and Art Jenkins on the violin. Every Friday night, the Jenkins boys walked down from the old mill carrying their instruments, played all night and walked the three miles home again in the dark. From time to time, the musicians were spelled off by Hughie Weir who loved to sit down and thump on the piano. The only thing he could play was a military two-step so we tried to make the breaks as short as possible. At midnight, a supper was served. All the women brought sandwiches or cake and the coffee was made in a huge urn. Afterwards, the party went on until two or three in the morning.

Saturday night, of course, was always 'Hockey Night in Canada'. Everyone crowded around the radio to listen to Foster Hewitt shout, 'He shoots! He *scores!*' Our favourite team was the Toronto Maple Leafs. In those days, radios were powered by a complicated arrangement of batteries. There was a 1,000-hour 'A' battery, which had to be filled with water before it could be used. Then there were three large 'B' batteries and two small 'C' batteries. One such set of batteries had to last the whole winter so the radio was used sparingly. Usually by the time the Stanley Cup play-offs came around, the batteries were running down and we had to huddle close to the speaker to hear the commentator.

One night a week we gathered at one of the boys' houses to play poker. Each player went to the game armed with a large box of Eddy's matches, as we couldn't afford to play for cash. There was always a bottle of homemade wine or beer to accompany the lunch. Henry Stone's house was a favourite meeting place because he made a particularly potent brand of dandelion wine, and one bottle proved to be more than enough on occasion.

For a change, I organized several debates and, as I had had previous experience, I was elected chairman. The subjects were usually frivolous, but one night I chose the topic 'Would a road be of benefit to Minaki or not?' It proved to be a hot one. Many people were against it, believing that it would change the nature of Minaki completely. Others were for it, as it would provide badly needed work during the off season. I finally ended up by vacating the chair and inviting Mr Charlton, the local Liberal representative, to take over. The meeting ended with a motion being passed, to draw up and present a petition to the provincial government to build a road. There is now a road from Kenora to Minaki. Whether it is of benefit to the village or not, I do not know. I like to think that the whole idea was started at that debate.

As November rolled on, the Indians started coming in with their furs from One Man Lake, White Dog and another reserve at Swan Lake. My knowledge of the Ojibway language kept increasing and soon I was able to conduct the trade with the trappers in their own language.

There was a small house at the back of our lot which we referred to as the Indian House. Here the trappers stayed overnight when they came in to trade. They tied up their dogs outside, helped themselves to our woodpile and made themselves comfortable.

Once or twice during the winter our outpost manager, Battiste Fisher, came in to replenish his stock. Battiste didn't drive a dog-team. He had a horse and sleigh and would show up sitting majestically on his sleigh, calmly smoking his pipe. As my knowledge of Ojibway increased and I was more at ease with it, I

decided to ask Battiste how the Indians were able to predict so
accurately just how severe the coming winter might be. He puffed
away on his pipe and shrugged his shoulders.

'Oh, come on, Battiste. Tell me. I've heard it's the amount of
rose hips on the wild rose bushes. And some say it's how much
food the squirrels accumulate or how thick the fur is on the
animals. How do the Indians really know?' I asked.

Battiste knocked his pipe against the woodpile near the door
and started to repack it. 'Well, Mr Ross, you are trying to learn
the Indian ways, so I'll tell you.' As we walked slowly away from
the house, he puffed away on his pipe, then turned to me with a
sober expression on his face and a twinkle in his eye.

'Indians watch very carefully. We notice the fur on the animals. We watch the birds. But if we see the white man chopping a
great pile of wood, the Indian knows for sure that we will have a
very cold winter.' Then he walked away leaving me roaring with
laughter.

Time slipped by quickly; soon we were out of winter and it
was spring, 1933.

Battiste Fisher was due to retire at the end of May, and the
Company decided to close One Man Lake as a year-round operation and run it instead as a wintering outpost. This was only good
business. Summer sales were low, as most of the local Indians and
their families went south to find summer guiding jobs at Minaki.
My job was to go to One Man Lake, take the inventory and close
up the buildings for the summer. At the end of May, with my
friend Jim Hayward as guide, we started out. Jim was an expert
canoeist and after lunch I asked him to let me steer. I was fed up
with being a bowman. At first, I steered a rather erratic course but
under Jim's highly caustic and frequently profane criticism, I
became more proficient.

Battiste had moved his family to his newly built house on the
reserve, had his furs already baled and was waiting for us. We
took inventory, then packed up the remaining hardware and dry
goods for return to Minaki. The groceries, we left in the warehouse, properly protected against mice. The windows were
boarded up, doors securely locked, and we were ready to go.
Battiste had his outboard motor boat tow the three freight canoes

and was accompanied by a gang of men to help cross the portages. Jim and I paddled back in our own canoe.

On the surface, everything at Minaki seemed to be going on as usual, but for some time I had detected an undercurrent of anxiety among the local people. Canada was still in the midst of the depression and many people were out of work. Some of those who still had jobs had to accept wage cuts. It was rumoured that Minaki Lodge would not open at all this season.

When we got back from One Man Lake, the news that the lodge would stay closed was official. Fortunately, the powers that be decided to keep on the maintenance staff and to operate the golf course and tennis courts as usual. None of the local people lost their jobs. The lodge closed for one season only.

That summer we noticed many young men riding the rails on the freight trains. They were not hobos or bums. They were young men travelling across the country, desperately looking for work. Whenever a freight train stopped at our station to allow the locomotive to take on water, we could be sure that ten or fifteen young fellows would dash up to the store asking for something to eat. Mr Yelland had laid down strict instructions that no one was to be turned away. Anyone who asked for food was to be given a half loaf of bread and a big hunk of cheese. I don't know whether this was Mr Yelland's own idea or if he was acting on instructions from Head Office. It was pitiful to see the looks of relief on the men's faces when they were given this small hand-out and to hear their stumbled thanks. If a man asked for a cigarette, I gave him a package of Fine Cut tobacco, which came complete with cigarette papers. They were only worth ten cents. As many of these young men were about my age, it made me conscious of how lucky I was, with my current salary of $35.00 a month, plus room and board.

Early in the summer season, we had a visit from Walter Black. He was one of the first of many efficiency experts hired by the Company to modernize our stores. Mr Black, a Glasgow man, had worked for the A & P Company in the United States and latterly, for the Abitibi Pulp and Paper Company in eastern Canada. His field was groceries. Unfortunately, he knew nothing at all about dry goods or hardware.

Soon he was busy re-arranging our store. Mr Yelland had

quite a battle with him to prevent him from reducing the space for dry goods. Mr Black wanted groceries everywhere. He insisted that we dress our two front windows once a week. This meant filling them with cases and cases of canned fruits and vegetables and placing large placards on the windows to advertise specials. The idea was fine but the only time I had available to change window displays was Sunday morning — my only time off. As a result I spent two or three hours Sunday morning, shifting cases around. I was provided with a set of paints and brushes and became adept at drawing price tickets.

There was one thing to which Bob Scott and I objected strenuously. Mr Black insisted that we wear black bow ties, white short jackets and long, white aprons. We were the epitome of Old Country counter-jumpers, but certainly not of Hudson's Bay traders. We were provided with two sets of these uniforms at the Company's expense but we had to pay for the laundering of them ourselves. And they became filthy very quickly. Bob and I had a long discussion about it one day and he went in to see Mr Yelland. We refused flatly to wear the uniform any longer. To our surprise, Mr Yelland agreed with us. He had wondered how long it would take for us to register our opposition. We dropped the new uniforms and, as Mr Black never returned to Minaki, nothing more was ever heard about it.

Orders came from Head Office that I was to take charge of One Man Lake outpost for the winter. My teeth had been troubling me for some time and I asked for and received permission to go to Winnipeg for treatment. Before doing so, I sat down with Mr Yelland and we made up a list of my winter requirements which would be ready to go on my return.

I was determined not to spend another winter in the bush without any source of entertainment so I negotiated with Roy Grellier, the boat-house man who sold radios on the side, for the purchase of a radio set. I had become an avid hockey fan and didn't want to miss any of the broadcasts. Grellier agreed to sell me a set with a deposit down and the balance to be paid monthly by Mr Yelland and charged to my account. Thus I became the proud possessor of a Westinghouse Console model radio which used the new type power-pack battery. It ran completely on drycell batteries and held an 'A' and three 'B's in a package about eighteen inches long by six inches wide and eight inches high. Its lifespan was about six months and it cost $7.50.

In Winnipeg, I registered at the Marlborough Hotel, which was the hotel used by the Company. As I was in on a medical trip, the Company paid the bill. Dr Christie's dental office was nearby on Portage Avenue and I went to see him first thing next morning. He and his family were regular summer visitors at Minaki and I had gotten to know them well. After examining my teeth, he told me there was a lot of work to be done and took me into another office where I waited while he was taking care of his regular appointments. Whenever he had some free minutes, back into the chair I went. I spent most of the week either in the chair or in the office. I ended up with sixteen gold fillings, six silver fillings and two extractions. He used anaesthetic only for the extractions. The bill came to $70.00. I can't say that I saw too much of the city on that trip, and for the next few months, I sent part of my monthly wages in to Dr Christie in Winnipeg in payment of the bill.

6

ONE MAN LAKE: WINTER 1933-34

Back in Minaki, we unloaded the annual carload of flour for the post. I then prepared to leave for One Man Lake. Mr Yelland had hired eighteen men to make the trip. There were twelve Indians from One Man Lake and six half-breeds from White Dog. The outpost freight was carried down to the government dock and loaded into a large wooden scow, along with our three Lac Seul freight canoes. Old Fred Cassie, one of the local boatmen, hitched up his gas-boat to the scow and we were off.

It was a lovely day with no wind and we had a fine passage crossing the open stretch of Big Sand Lake before getting to the first portage at White Dog. The scow was unloaded and Fred left us to return to Minaki. The men set to work, portaging the freight around the sheer drop of the first falls. They were experts at their tasks and carried an average load of two hundred pounds per trip. They used leather tumplines or portage straps which were made of two long leather straps attached to a broad headpiece. The two straps were tied around a sack or bale and adjusted so that when the headpiece was placed across the forehead, the load lay in the small of the back. Then further bales were piled on at the back of the neck, giving a perfect counterbalance. The men trotted over the portage with their full load, dumped it and trotted back for another load. We had everything carried over and made camp on the other side.

The next day was spent getting around the following two rapids. We used a slightly different procedure when we hit these two rapids. The canoes were only half unloaded. Then, with our half-loads still on board, we ran the canoes down the white water.

What an exhilarating adventure that was; one more thing I had dreamt of doing. Few men can handle a paddle as expertly as Indians. They knew exactly what to do at the bowman's call as we approached jagged rocks.

The second night, we camped just below the second rapids. We didn't carry tents with us but slept on the ground under the freight canoes. The large tarpaulins used to cover the freight were spread out on the ground. Using them as groundsheets, we wrapped ourselves in blankets and pulled the balance of the tarps over us. Even if it rained, the overturned canoes gave us sufficient protection from the elements.

Cooking was a simple operation. A large ten-gallon pail was set to boil over the fire. Everything went into it — bacon, beans, potatoes. While the men were carrying the loads over the portages, I passed the time wandering in the bush with my shotgun, or fishing in the river. Whatever I bagged, whether it was a jackfish, partridge or rabbit, it was added to the pot. Soon, we could fish almost anything out of that pot. The third day, we paddled up the White Dog River, portaged over into Goshawk Lake and camped on an island halfway up. In the evening the men went deer hunting and shot a fine buck.

Next morning, I ran into trouble. Charlie Savoyard, the leader of the White Dog men, announced that unless I increased their daily wages, they would not go any further. I hadn't expected anything like this, but managed not to show my dismay. I quickly figured that, if I had to, I could make do with the twelve Indians from One Man Lake. I didn't know the bunch from White Dog but decided I would call their bluff. All the men stopped working to see how I handled it.

Casually I rolled a cigarette, lit it with a brand from the fire, looked straight at Charlie and said, 'Sorry, Charlie, you agreed to the wages offered before we left the post. If you don't want to work, that's fine with me.' I turned my back on them and wandered down to the shore while the men huddled together, talking over this development. When they made no further comments or moves to go back to work, I divided the twelve into three groups, four men to a canoe. They finished loading up and as I indicated that we get started, Charlie jumped up and shouted, 'Hey, what about us?', realizing for the first time that his bluff had been called.

'You had better get back to White Dog, Charlie. You don't want to work. Fine. We can manage without you,' I said, firmly.

'But, how are we going to get off the island and get back to White Dog?' he spluttered. 'We don't have a canoe.' By now, he and his friends were visibly anxious and sorry they had started the whole thing.

'That is your problem. You should have thought of that before you tried to hold me up.' As I walked to the waiting canoe, Charlie held a hurried conclave with his crew and sheepishly announced that they had decided to work for the agreed wages.

As I hesitated, he assured me that they wouldn't give me any trouble and that they weren't really serious. 'O.K., then get aboard and let's not have any more of this nonsense.' As we pulled away from shore, I heaved a great sigh of relief. The rest of the trip continued without incident and the White Dog men worked just as hard as always.

Three days later, we crossed the last portage into One Man Lake. There was a favourable wind blowing from the south and Cornelius MacDonald, one of the One Man Lake Indians said, 'Good. No paddling today, Mr Ross. Today, we sail!' Six long spruce poles were cut in the bush and trimmed. One pole was lashed as a crosspiece near the top of a second one. This was installed in the front of each canoe. There was a hole in the middle of the forward thwart and a step under it for just such use. A blanket was lashed to the crosspiece and the two lower ends tied to tumplines which were held by a man sitting in the middle of the canoe. While the rest of us relaxed, the canoe sailed across the lake, controlled by one man handling the sail and a steersman. In about three hours, we arrived at the outpost, and I had the freight all unloaded into the store instead of the warehouse. The six White Dog men left in one canoe; the other two canoes were put up on racks until the following spring.

There was a lot of work to do and I set to immediately. The house was a large one so I decided to use it as a combination store and living quarters. There was no point in heating two buildings, especially when I was the one who had to cut the wood.

*Freighting into One Man Lake, Autumn
1933. Charles and Gus Savoyard (left and
centre), brothers of Mrs. S. A. Taylor whose
husband was post manager at White Dog
for many years.*

Baking bannock on the way to One Man Lake.

I divided the house into two with a partition. At one end, I installed the counter and shelving from the old store. Then I unpacked the merchandise, checked it and put it on display. I was ready for business.

This time, there was some furniture: a bed, table and two kitchen chairs, an armchair and a huge oak sideboard with a mirror on the back. There was also a good cast-iron cookstove and a Carron heater which took bigger logs and retained its heat much longer than a tin airtight heater. I knocked down the old warehouse and an old horsebarn, sawed up the lumber and used it as firewood for the cookstove.

Over the years, most of the good wood had been cleared around the post so I had to walk quite a distance into the bush to find green birch for winter heating. I continued the practice I had started at my Long Legged Outpost, of taking an axe with me when I went walking in the evening. I missed Caesar during these treks but he was too old to have made the trip and I had to leave him at the main post.

One of the first things I did was to set up my radio. I strung up an aerial from the store to the house and ran an iron rod into the earth for the required grounding. It was a pleasure to sit back in my armchair in the evening and listen to some good music, serials like 'One Man's Family' and 'The Green Hornet' and, more importantly, news of the outside world.

The Indians were fascinated by the radio. They all loved square dance and country music. Once a week, there was a two-hour radio program from Chicago called 'The Country Barn Dance', whose principal characters were Skyland Scottie and Lulubelle. I invited some of the Indians over one night to hear the program. After examining the radio, they sat themselves on the floor and listened quietly, tapping their feet in time to the music. When the program was over, they waited until they heard the program of the classical music that followed. They didn't care much for the high soprano and, rising to their feet, thanked me and left, murmuring their wonderment at this strange type of gramophone.

There was no sense of isolation at One Man Lake. The post was on the mainland, right next to the reserve, and every day there were customers in the store. No longer was I cut off from everyone and everything during freeze-up and break-up.

Just before freeze-up, Kitchee Jacob shot a moose, decided to throw a party and I was invited. I dug out my blue suit, polished my brown, pointed-toe oxfords and donned a white shirt and tie. Since the party was for Kitchee Jacob's grandson's birthday, I took an appropriate gift of blue sateen material for the child; and sugar, tea and tobacco for Kitchee and his wife. He believed in doing things in proper style. I, being the *Ogema,* or boss, had a special place set for me at a table with a little piece of white table oilcloth on which rested a tin plate, an enamel mug, a fork, knife and spoon. As guest of honour, I was served the choicest part of the moose — the nose — boiled. I could hardly look at the horrible, glutinous, grey chunk that was on my plate, but I ate it. It would have been a serious breach of manners to have done otherwise. Everyone had a wonderful time. The Indians sat on the floor, crowded along the walls, and enjoyed the juicy moosemeat steaks and piles of ribs that were set before them by the women. Huge piles of bannock were heaped on the table, along with fruit pies of all kinds. Lashings of strong, sweet tea followed and then someone tuned up a fiddle and the dancing began.

Square dance followed square dance and I tried to dance with every woman, starting with Kitchee Jacob's wife. I even felt confident enough to call a few figures. When we were all tuckered out from dancing, the fiddler would strike up a stirring tune in jig time. An Indian took his place in the centre of the floor and proceeded to do an intricate step dance, beating time rapidly to music. The rhythm was taken up by everyone sitting against the walls, by beating their moccasined feet on the floor. When one man was tired, his place was taken by another who tried to duplicate and improve on the predecessor's step dancing. As he went through his gyrations in the middle of the floor, a woman joined him and quietly danced in a slow circle around him, her feet barely moving in a slow shuffling step. This was the famous 'Red River Jig'.

Everyone had to do a turn and when it came to me, I jumped up and did a variation of the Highland Fling, which was well received by the gathering. The feasting and dancing went on until the wee, small hours of the morning, when I returned home and stumbled into bed, completely worn out.

Soon the Indians were bringing in their furs. They were a good group to deal with and the trade was successful. The women kept busy making deerskin moccasins with bead trimmings in the traditional Ojibway patterns of flowers and leaves. I encouraged them and bought all they offered for sale. The workmanship was first-class and the moccasins were popular with the tourists at Minaki.

As someone was always making a trip into the main post, I received mail much more frequently than at Long Legged Outpost. Occasionally, I hired a dog-team to go down for supplies and sent out any fur I had on hand. I was always too busy to go myself.

That winter, my diet was more varied. In the fall, there were lots of partridges, ducks and fresh fish. In the winter someone always brought in a choice piece of moose or deer meat for me. I also brought a greater selection of canned meat and vegetables for my own use. In my order, I had asked for one case of assorted breakfast cereal and one case of assorted tinned fruit. Mr Yelland had taken the opportunity to get rid of some of his slow-moving stock and my two assorted cases turned out to be one case of Shredded Wheat and one case of a cheap variety of Singapore pineapple. Needless to say, I haven't eaten either of them since.

I decided to have a go at baking my own bread. I had watched my mother countless times and knew the mechanics. Fast-rising yeast hadn't come on the market. Instead there was a brand called Royal Yeast which came in six small cakes to the package. The only thing wrong with it was that it took about twelve hours to raise the dough. This was all right in the autumn when I could leave it overnight to rise but in the middle of winter, there was a chance of it freezing. I adopted the simple expedient of taking the dough to bed with me. I wrapped the basin in my sheep-lined coat and put it under the blankets at the foot of the bed. Sometimes it didn't rise completely but I didn't have too many failures. Although the bread was a little close-grained at times, it tasted wonderful to me after years of nothing but bannock. I baked a half-dozen loaves at a time, once I had mastered

One Man Lake Outpost, 1933.

Kitchee Jacob scraping a moose-hide, One Man Lake.

H. M. Ross, and a partial view of the wood pile.

the mysteries of baking with yeast. During the winter, I set them outside to freeze. If I made a few pies at the same time, I could plan on baking every two weeks.

One of the few Indians who had a good potato garden was Kitchee Jacob and I purchased several sacks from him. I kept them upstairs in the attic along with my supply of Carnation Milk. Wrapped well in tarpaulins to prevent frost damage, they sat between the two stove pipes which went up through the attic and the roof. I usually boiled a fair-sized pot of potatoes, had them boiled the first day and then as hash browns until the pot was finished.

When the winter trapping season ended and business slackened off in the store, it was back to the woodpile again. I was determined that there would be a good stock of seasoned firewood on hand next fall for either myself or my replacement. I borrowed a toboggan and almost every day, went into the bush to cut down a good-sized birch tree and chop it into logs. As it was downhill most of the way, it was much easier to tie three or four-foot lengths onto the toboggan and drag them back to the post than it was to carry them on my shoulders, as I had done the previous fall.

Not far away, there lived an old Indian named Thomas Big-Blood. He was too old to do any extensive trapping so he came over to visit me almost every day. He spoke very good English and we became friends. I tried out my Ojibway on him and Thomas corrected me where necessary, helping me to build my vocabulary. While I was becoming quite fluent and could carry on a simple conversation, there were still a number of aspects of the language that eluded me. Among other things, the old Indian told me many of the stories and legends of his people. These were mainly about Kitchee Manitou, the Great Spirit, and Nana Bousho, the mischievous spirit who went about playing tricks on everyone.

Shortly after Christmas, I had written and submitted a short story on Kitchee Jacob's party to the editor of *The Beaver,* then the Company's staff magazine. My story was accepted and printed. Greatly heartened by my success, I decided to write a series of stories on the legends which Old Thomas had told me. To my chagrin, my first story was returned with a note from the editor saying that he regretted he could not print it. The explanation was that the Indian legends varied in different parts of the country and were too controversial a subject to print. Some time later, when I was visiting Winnipeg, I picked up a book entitled *Legends of the Swampy Cree;* the tales were practically identical to those told to me by old Thomas Big-Blood.

Muskrat trapping season opened on 15 April, and this spring the Ontario Department of Game and Fisheries decided to have an open season on beaver. Beaver trapping had been closed for a number of years to allow the depleted stocks to rebuild. Now there was a good crop of both muskrat and beaver and trading was brisk.

The long, balmy spring evenings were too warm and pleasant to spend inside. I went on long walks around the reserve, talking to the people and watching them as they went about their business. Some of the men were busy patching and repainting their canoes in preparation for the coming open water. Old Thomas tanned a moosehide. The women tended to their cooking on open fires outside the homes.

There was the sound of tom-toms in the air, the beating cadence rising and falling and quickening in pitch. One evening I decided to investigate and ended up at Battiste Fisher's house. Inside, two teams of four men were lined up along each side of a blanket spread on the floor. The room was crowded with Indians, sitting or standing along the walls. The air was tense with excitement and low murmurings.

The team leader on each side held a long willow wand in his hand; each man held a handful of wooden markers. Bets were placed with the markers. At the start of the tom-tom, a man on the first team went through a series of motions with four pieces of leather shaped like moccasins on the blanket in front of him. He slid his hand under one moccasin, then under another, then the third and finally the last. Members of the other team watched him closely. When the tom-tom beat quickened, he stopped and looked at his opponent. Battiste told me that the leader of the first team had hidden a lead bullet under one of the pieces of leather; the leader of the opposite team had to guess which moccasin covered the bullet. After tentatively moving his wand from one moccasin to another, looking into his opponent's eyes for any telltale sign, he gave a shout and flicked one of the moccasins away with the willow wand. If the lead bullet was under that moccasin, his team won their bets; otherwise the bets were paid to the other team.

I didn't see any money change hands, but Battiste explained that the bets could be anything that the winning team accepted —12-gauge shells, 30.30 bullets or muskrat traps. I have been told that dog-teams, harnesses, toboggans, canoes and even furs would change hands during these games as the excitement grew. The Indians loved to gamble.

Just before the end of May, Jim Woodward, the resident game warden at Minaki, came put-putting up the lake to check my fur books against my furs in hand. Everything was in order. It was time to close up the post and return to Minaki for another summer season.

7

MINAKI: SUMMER 1934

I had learned a lot the past winter. My command of the Indian language and my trading techniques had improved greatly, since I was dealing with the trappers every day. But I also spent a good deal of time trying to solve my romantic dilemma and, unfortunately, hadn't come to any satisfactory conclusion.

For the past two summers a young Winnipeg schoolteacher, Beatrice Dingle, had been my constant companion. We were tennis partners and a regular twosome at the dances. During the winter I admitted to myself that she was the girl I wanted for my wife. But what was I to do about Peggy Miller, the girl I had become engaged to before leaving Scotland? We had agreed that we would be married when I returned home in 1935. It wouldn't be fair to ask Bea to marry me until Peggy had released me from our long engagement. In the past year, our letters had been few and far between, and were more the kind sent from one friend to another than love letters. I was really in a pickle.

They say that fate takes care of fools and lovers and it certainly took a hand. A few days before Bea was due to arrive for her annual holiday at Holst Point, I received a letter from Peggy. It wasn't a case of 'absence makes the heart grow fonder' with us, but rather 'out of sight, out of mind'. She had gone to London to work and had met a detective-sergeant who wanted to marry her. By return mail, and without mentioning a word about Bea, I sat down and replied that I understood perfectly and wished them both the best of luck. Then I went out and celebrated.

With the approach of the tourist season, Bob Scott began thinking that the summer work was too much for him. He had served in World War I and his health had been damaged by poisonous gas. He decided to pack it in at the end of June. The Company sent down a replacement for him, a young university student from Winnipeg named Bert McNaughton. Bert was to work in the store for the summer and return to school in the fall. He was slight in stature and I'm sure that during the first two or three weeks, the work must have almost killed him. But he had guts and never said that any job was too much for him. He always did his share and it wasn't long before he could handle the incoming freight just as well as I did.

During the summers at Minaki, I had a room in the boss's house, which I shared with Horace, his son, when he was home. But it was too small for three people and Mr Yelland decided that Bert and I could use the three-roomed suite upstairs above the warehouse, where we each had a room of our own and were responsible for keeping it clean. We ate our meals, as usual, with the Yellands. Since the suite had a private entrance, no longer did we worry about being in bed on time. We were free to come and go as we pleased. Most mornings, we put on our swim suits, ran down to the lake for a wash and swim before breakfast. It was great to be on our own and we quickly became friends.

Bea finally arrived in early July. One night, as we sat on a blanket on the rocks overlooking the lake at Holst Point, I asked her to marry me. At the look of astonishment on her face, my heart sank. Although we hadn't actually spoken about it, I was sure she felt the same way as I did. I must have looked crestfallen because she took my hand and explained that it was her second proposal that week. Now it was my turn to look astonished. 'A City Man!' I thought. 'I won't stand a chance against him.' But apparently her first suitor, while he had a job with a small salary, had very little chance of promotion in the present economic climate. The proposal was so vague that Bea had come down to think it over. My question had complicated matters even more. She looked so unhappy that I persuaded her to put the whole business out of her mind for the time being.

'Why don't we start out as we left off last summer? Let's be friends again and enjoy your holidays.' She agreed and we had a wonderful month together. True to my word, I never mentioned my proposal.

Beatrice Dingle and Hugh Ross at Holst Point, 1934.

Western Canada Pictorial Index.

A view of Holst Point, Minaki, 1927.

The night before she left, we went back to the rock at Holst Point and had a long talk. 'Thanks for not pressuring me, Hugh. It's been a wonderful summer. I think I should tell you what I've decided to do.' I held my breath. 'I'll go home tomorrow and think things over and I promise I'll be back in two weeks to give you my answer. O.K.?'

I agreed, but it was a long two weeks, and if the boss was sometimes exasperated with my day-dreaming, he controlled himself admirably. But the time passed and when she arrived, she put my fears to rest. Yes. She would marry me.

'Look, Hugh,' she said, 'it's not going to be all that easy. My mother doesn't mind. She thinks it's all very romantic. But my father almost went out of his mind. He can't or won't understand why I would leave Winnipeg to go out into the bush to marry someone he has never even met. He wants to give you the once-over.'

I could understand her father's apprehension. There were no amenities in the bush and life would be almost primitive in comparison with what Bea had been used to.

'Do you think you can get away for a week or so and come to Winnipeg to meet my family? Mind you,' she added with a smile, 'no matter what my father says, I am going to marry you.'

I assured her that I would get the time off and added that, in fact, this was necessary, as I had to get the Company's permission to marry. I still had a year to go to complete my apprenticeship and under the Company's rules, permission wasn't granted until one became a post manager.

Right after Labour Day, I left Minaki for Winnipeg and checked in, as usual, at the Marlborough Hotel. Bright and early next morning, I presented myself at Hudson's Bay House. My district manager was out of town but the accountant told me that Mr Parsons, the fur trade commissioner, wanted to see me. Now what, I wondered. Marian Ross, the commissioner's private secretary, was a close friend of Bea's. They belonged to the same bridge club, played tennis together at the Canoe Club, and shared confidences. After a short wait, she came to escort me to Mr Parson's office. 'Don't look so worried,' she said. 'Everything is going to be all right.'

As I shook hands with him, Mr Parsons said, 'Well, Ross, it seems that you are stirring up a good deal of interest at Hudson's Bay House. So you want to get married, eh?'

I was surprised that he knew about it already. It seemed that my future father-in-law, in his agitation over his daughter's proposed marriage to a complete stranger, had been making inquiries about my position and prospects with the Company. These inquiries had been directed to his friends who were members of the Canadian Committee of the Hudson's Bay Company. In due course, they had filtered down to the fur trade commissioner.

Mr Parsons went on to explain the Company's rules and regulations regarding marriage and pointed out that I still had a year of my apprenticeship to go before I would be eligible for a post of my own. He added, however, that my record was good and that he could see nothing to prevent my getting a post. So I could go ahead with my wedding arrangements.

Greatly encouraged by his remarks, I ventured to ask him whether my future might go in any other direction than being a post manager. 'What do you mean?' he asked, looking very puzzled.

'Well, I was given to understand when I joined the Company, that the only way to get ahead was to become a bookkeeper or an accountant,' I explained.

He looked at me for a minute and said, 'I don't know who gave you that advice, Ross, but it's bad advice. If I want a bookkeeper or an accountant, all I have to do is place an advertisement in one of the local newspapers. Within half an hour, my office would be swamped with university graduates who are desperately looking for a job. What this Company needs are traders. Men who sell merchandise and buy fur. No accountant can show a profit unless we have traders in the organization.'

He paused. 'Judging by the reports on you, you have the makings of a good trader. If you want my advice, my boy, and if you want to get on in this Company, stick to trading.'

He then advised me that I was to return to One Man Lake as outpost manager for the coming winter. I was to come and see him again in the spring, at which time all postings for the following year were drawn up and agreed upon. I reminded him that I was due six months' leave of absence the next summer.

'We'll decide on that when you come to see me. In the meantime, it's all right to go ahead and get engaged to your young lady but don't set a firm date for the wedding until you've seen me in the spring.'

I suppose, in this day and age, that it will appear strange that I had to request permission to get married, but it was a matter of simple logic. At that time, there were no separate married quarters for staff at most of the Company's posts. It was fine to have a single apprentice clerk stay in the house with the post manager and his family, but it would have been out of the question to expect the post manager to have another married couple sharing the same home.

After lunch, I set out in great fear and trepidation for my next appointment — my future father-in-law.

Guy V. Dingle had been a partner in the firm of Dingle and Stewart. They made candies, chocolate bars and chocolates, including a well-known brand of chocolates, 'Melba'. Like so many others, the firm had gone under during the depression and he was now working with the Manufacturer's Life Insurance Company. He had been a city man all his life and other than playing his regular golf games and going out to shoot partridge in the Interlake District each fall, he was not an outdoors type.

When I formally asked for his daughter's hand in marriage, as one did in those days, he put me through a long cross-examination of my past, background and future expectations. He frankly admitted that he was scared stiff at the thought of his daughter going out into the bush to live among Indians and half-breeds. But, as he had received favourable reports from Hudson's Bay House and my prospects seemed good, he gave our marriage his blessing. 'Knowing my daughter,' he grumbled, 'I don't suppose it would make any difference if I gave my consent or not. She's of age and if she's made up her mind to marry you, she'll do it, no matter what I say.'

He invited me home for dinner that evening, where I met the rest of the family. Mrs Dingle suggested that I spend the rest of my holidays with them, so I checked out of the hotel. With everything seeming to go our way, my worries subsided and Bea and I had a wonderful time. We wandered all over the city, window shopping and usually ending up for a meal at Moore's Restaurant on Portage Avenue where we enjoyed their specialty, Winnipeg Goldeye. Bea introduced me to all her friends; we danced at the Canoe Club and saw the latest 'talkies' at the picture house. We agreed not to announce our engagement officially until Christmas when Bea would come down to Minaki. I would arrange to come in from One Man Lake to meet her, and we would stay either at Mr Yelland's house or at Holst Point.

8

ONE MAN LAKE: WINTER 1934-35

Back at Minaki, I packed my own supply of trading goods and this time I hired my own freighters — all from One Man Lake. We set out early in October and, after portaging at White Dog Falls, we took a different route to avoid the small portages we had made the previous year. Instead of going up the White Dog River, we continued along the Winnipeg River until we came to Deer Falls, beyond which the English River joined the Winnipeg. After portaging there, we proceeded east along the English River. The weather was fine and the wind, favourable. We set our sails and enjoyed the trip as the canoes skimmed over the water. Although the distance covered was greater, we were able to cut one and a half days off the time, thus ensuring a considerable saving in freighting costs.

For the next few days, I unpacked, checked, marked and displayed my merchandise. Trade was brisk and there seemed to be quite a bit of money floating around, although there were few men to be seen during the day. My curiosity got the better of me and I cornered Battiste Fisher the first time he came into the store.

'What's going on?' I asked. 'Where is everybody?'

'Oh, they are away fishing. They are all out tending their nets in the morning.' I knew that Bud Hatch, a commercial fisherman from Kenora, was running a fishing operation on Big Sand Lake, north of Minaki. He had a warehouse and an ice-house near White Dog Falls. But I also knew that it was impossible to fish One Man Lake and make a living with the current prices being received on the market for whitefish and pickerel. 'What are you fishing for?' I asked.

Battiste Fisher, post manager at One Man Lake until retirement in 1933, with sturgeon. (The spelling 'Battiste' appears on all Company documents.)

Indians preparing the sturgeon for transport to Kenora.

'*Kitchee Namay*,' Battiste answered, with a grin. This was a new one on me. *Namaygosh* or lake trout, I was familiar with. But *Kitchee Namay*?

' Oh sure,' he said. '*Kitchee Namay* is sturgeon.' All I knew about sturgeon was that it was a fabled fish caught in the river Volga in Russia and that it produced large quantities of expensive caviar. In Britain it was a 'royal' fish; if you caught one, you had to offer it to the monarch.

'Come on now, Battiste,' I said. 'You're making fun of me. What are you really catching?'

Battiste laughed and replied emphatically, 'Sturgeon! Tomorrow morning, I will take you over to see, when I go with my two sons.'

Early next morning, we set out across the lake to the fishing camp. It was situated in a large, shallow, almost land-locked bay. Indians were already arriving from their nets and in their canoes were the largest fish I had ever seen. They were all at least four feet long, as this was the minimum length prescribed by the Ontario Game and Fisheries Department. They had no scales but a rough, leathery skin and their mouths were like huge, underslung pouches; they looked to me like gigantic suckers.

The sturgeon were still alive. Instead of killing them, the Indians ran a long length of cod-line through the gills and out the mouth of each fish and tied it in a loop. The other end was tied to a tree near the shore. Then the fins were cut off and the still-live fish thrown back into the shallow waters of the bay. Battiste explained that this was the only way that they could keep the fish fresh. When they had accumulated an airplane-load, two men paddled down to White Dog and asked Bud Hatch to send in an aircraft. Bud went down to Minaki in his motorboat, telegraphed Kenora, and the next day a Norseman aircraft would fly in to pick up a load of sturgeon. On the morning of the plane's arrival, the fish were killed and dressed. In a few short hours, the fish were weighed, paid for and on their way to market. Mr Hatch had set up this operation the previous spring. In season, he bought the caviar as well; it was stripped from the fish into large bath-tubs and then sieved through coarse screens into pails. I don't remember how much he paid per pound for the sturgeon, but I do recall that he paid $1.00 a pound for the caviar. This was good money in the pockets of the Indians and good for sales at the post.

The smaller sturgeon were put back into the lake as soon as they were removed from the nets but several which did not quite make the minimum measurement of four feet were kept by the natives and smoked. The fish was palatable although a bit oily, and I did enjoy the smoked sturgeon cheeks which were, in the Indians' estimation, the best part. Later on, I tasted bannock made with sturgeon roe mixed through it, but I didn't care too much for that.

Time passed and almost before I knew it, I was once again in the middle of the fur-buying season. Then, it was the middle of December. I made arrangements with Cornelius MacDonald for the hire of his dog-team to make the trip to Minaki for Christmas. I had received the necessary permission from the Company to do this, and Mr and Mrs Yelland had kindly invited Bea and me to stay with them.

Battiste Fisher had agreed to look after the fires at the post during my absence so that nothing would freeze. Early on the morning of 22 December, I hitched up my hired dog-team and set out for White Dog. The weather was good and the trail packed hard. At first I had a little difficulty with the dogs. Indian dogs do not take kindly to a white man driving them, but after a few judicious cracks of the whip to let them know who was boss, they straightened out and got down to the business at hand.

The first day was completed without incident. I arrived at White Dog before dark and spent the night there at the house of John McDonald, a native who worked as a guide in Minaki during the summer. From White Dog south to Minaki I wasn't too sure of the trail. In order to avoid the rapids at White Dog and the weak ice nearby, the trail swung considerably to the west and then south through Swan Lake Reserve. I questioned John at great length about this and he assured me that I would have no difficulty.

'Just follow the trail through the reserve, along the bank of the White Dog River to its mouth. Here the trail takes a wide loop across the Winnipeg River,' he said. 'It is well beaten down. Just stay with it because it picks up the spots where the ice is good.' He sipped his tea and continued. 'Once you get across the river, Mr Ross, the trail goes through the bush and across a chain of small lakes to Swan Lake Reserve. Lots of Indians have been over the trail lately. You can't miss it!'

John stopped, lit his pipe and then warned, 'There is only one place about eight miles from here where there is a fork in the trail. Take the right hand fork. Don't forget — the right hand fork. You can't miss it. It's the more beaten down trail of the two.'

So next morning, I again hitched up the dogs and started out. Everything was as Johnny had described. I got over the Winnipeg River safely and onto a good trail going straight through the bush. After about two hours, sure enough, there was a split in the trail. I looked at the two trails closely. The right hand branch was heavily beaten down, so I followed it.

I drove steadily along for another couple of hours, hitting a good pace. Suddenly in the middle of the portage the trail stopped cold. The dogs were jumping around excitedly. I looked around at the unmistakable evidence in the snow; a couple of moose had been killed and butchered there. No wonder the trail was so beaten down. The Indians had taken the heavy loads of meat to White Dog. Johnny hadn't known about this and couldn't have warned me.

There was nothing to do but backtrack to that fork in the trail, which would take another two hours. Since it was obvious now that I wouldn't reach Minaki that night, all I could hope for was that I could get to Swan Lake and spend the night there instead of having to sleep out in the bush.

When I arrived at the forks, I took the other branch. In due course, I came to the right-hand turn which Johnny had advised me about and followed it. It was a long, hard slog before I spotted a light in the distance and made for it. It was the only light to be seen and I was thankful that there was even that one; usually the Swan Lake Indians all went down to the track at Christmas time.

Arriving at the house, I was greeted by the loud barking of dogs which were tethered up all around the house. An Indian immediately opened the door to shout the dogs down; he was very surprised to see me standing there. He invited me to spend the night and made me welcome. The shack was filled with trappers who had come down from their hunting grounds and were going on to Minaki the next day. Their gear was piled in one corner and they sat around the stove smoking. A large bundle about six feet long, covered by a tarpaulin, was stretched along the far wall. They made a space for me between it and the stove. After taking care of the dogs and cooking a meal, we shared a cigarette and discussed the trapping. Then I unwrapped my blankets, stretched out on the floor and immediately went to sleep. It had been a long, tiring day.

When I awoke, I discovered I had moved away from the hot stove during the night and was lying alongside the bundle. I let the Indians make their breakfast first, as I wanted them to hit the trail ahead of me. They would travel faster than I could and the knowledge that their dogs were ahead would give my team an incentive to pull harder. They finished and went about loading their toboggans. The last item to be removed was the bundle. When they took off the tarpaulin, I was horrified to discover that I had slept peacefully all night beside a corpse. One of the trappers had died and they were taking him down to the track to be buried. The shock took away my appetite. I didn't feel much like cooking — even less like eating breakfast that morning.

It was a short, easy run from Swan Lake to Minaki and I arrived about noon, just in time to feed my dogs, turn over my furs to Mr Yelland, and get myself spruced up to meet the afternoon train from Winnipeg.

Bea stepped off the train, accompanied by Horace and Jeff Yelland and their girl-friends. It was a happy reunion and as we walked up to the house from the station, Bea quietly slipped me a small package that she had brought with her. I don't suppose there are too many young women who can claim that they purchased their own engagement ring.

'You should have seen the saleslady's face, Hugh. She was one of those prim women with blue-rinsed hair. She got very upset when she realized that I was actually going to buy my own engagement ring.' Bea laughed as she related the rest of her adventure. 'It was really very funny. She grumbled about how shameless the young people of today are. I never explained and she grudgingly took the money. But she did a lovely job on the wrapping, didn't she?'

Before dinner that night, I slipped the ring on Bea's finger, and during the house party that followed, glasses were raised frequently to toast our engagement.

On Christmas Day, we all slept in later than usual. After lunch, Bea and I walked around visiting friends, especially Skipper Holst who was delighted to hear our news. He took all the credit for our engagement and poured out bumpers of Schnapps for everyone in the lodge, to drink to our happiness.

That evening, we sat down with the Yellands and shared their Christmas dinner — roast turkey and all the trimmings. As we ate, I looked around the table at all the happy faces. Then I looked across at Bea. She and Mrs Yelland were discussing the problems of living so far from civilization. Soon we too would be sharing this kind of celebration. But in our own home.

We walked up to the village hall to join in the dancing. The news of our coming wedding had already gone round the village. If we had accepted all the drinks that were offered to us, we wouldn't have been in any condition to participate in the dancing, which went on until the early morning hours.

With the sound of good wishes ringing in our ears, we returned to Mr Yelland's house. Most of the party went off to bed, but since Bea had to catch the 5:30 a.m. train back to Winnipeg, we spent the remaining hours talking and making plans. Bea said she could catch up on her sleep on the train. Reluctantly, I kissed her goodbye and watched the train pull out. I walked back up the hill, hitched up my dogs and set out on the return journey to One Man Lake.

The weather was brisk and clear and the dogs were in fine fettle after their long rest. My load of supplies wasn't large, so we kept up a good pace. By late afternoon, I reached White Dog where I spent the night with Johnny McDonald. When I told him about taking the wrong trail and ending up at the moose kill, he thought it was a great joke and laughed mightily.

By morning, the weather had turned mild and it started to snow. I plodded on. Halfway across Goshawk Lake, it was snow-ing steadily. I put on my snow-shoes and walked ahead of the dogs. It slowed me down considerably and by the time I had crossed the last portage onto One Man Lake, it was getting dark. Fortunately the snow had stopped. I had great difficulty in keeping to the trail, which was almost invisible under the blanket of new snow. The lead dog was tired and, not smart to begin with, kept losing the trail on the big lake. Every time this happened, I had to circle around ahead of the dogs, feeling for the hard trail underneath the new, loose snow.

Off the trail there was slush under the snow, which froze to the bottom of the toboggan. Each time this happened, I had to turn it on its side, scrape the slush off with my axe, heave the toboggan back onto the trail and get the dogs going again. It got darker and darker. The lead dog continually wandered away from the hard trail into the slush and I continually had to scrape the toboggan. I could see the lights in the houses on the hill but they didn't seem to get any closer.

I finally reached the post, utterly exhausted. The dogs collapsed on the ground, panting from the exertion of the trek. It had taken us six hours to cross that damned lake and they were as tired as I was. I wanted nothing more than to stagger into bed. But first, I had to take care of the dogs, unpack my supplies and make sure that everything at the post was all right. Thank goodness the house fire was on and the house was warm. Eventually I crawled into bed and slept like the dead until noon the next day.

In mid-January, a passing Indian brought me a bundle of mail from Minaki. Included in the bundle was a letter from District Office containing a new contract. It stated that as of 1 January 1935, I officially had the title of 'outpost manager' at a new salary of $50.00 per month. They also enclosed a cheque for $25.00 as a bonus for the previous winter's operation.

Springtime was always woodcutting time. Whether it was carelessness or the fact that my mind was on other things (like Bea and our coming wedding), I wasn't concentrating on the job. Instead of biting into the wood, my axe glanced off the still-frozen birch tree I was chopping down and bit into my right foot. I noticed a long, diagonal cut in my moccasin rubber, but there was no pain. I cursed my carelessness because I would have to buy a new pair of moccasin rubbers, and continued to chop the tree.

As I bent to pick up smaller branches I had cut off, I noticed blood oozing from the cut. It still didn't hurt, but I made my way back to the post as quickly as possible, leaving a trail of blood in the snow. At the house, I stripped off the moccasin rubber, moccasin, duffle oversock and three pairs of woollen socks. All were soaked with blood. Thoroughly alarmed at the sight, I wiped the blood away and discovered a deep cut about one and a half inches long in the fleshy part of the foot at the base of my big toe. I tried wiggling the toe. It wiggled so I decided there wasn't any damage done to the bone or tendon. The many layers of footwear had saved me from what could have been a very serious accident.

I staunched the flow of blood and realized the gash had to be stitched up. No bandage would keep it together. Not looking forward to the job ahead, I got out a bottle of whisky that I kept for special occasions. This definitely could be classified as a special occasion. I poured a lot of whisky over the cut. It burned like hell, but I thought it would be as effective an antiseptic as any. Besides, I didn't have anything else. Then, I sloshed an equal amount down my throat, sterilized a needle over a match and taking a deep breath and another drink from the bottle, stitched the thing up. When I finished the sewing, I poured some more whisky over the wound again for good measure. I had no medical supplies in the house at all, except Band-aids. I tore one of my few remaining white shirts into strips, bandaged up my foot and hobbled around the post for the next couple of weeks, using two corn brooms as crutches. Every so often, I changed the dressing, looking for signs of infection. But the whisky did the trick and eventually the cut healed. I still have the scar to remind me.

One sunny afternoon in early May, I went for a walk along the shore of the river where it entered the lake. The snow had gone and the air was filled with the songs of birds. It was that time of the year when the woods were alive with new growth. As I listened to the conversation of two squirrels in a birch tree, I was aware of another, rather strange sound. Sort of a hissing noise. Quietly, I walked up a rocky slope, following the sound and finally locating the source. I drew back from the sight in disgust. In a hole were hundreds of snakes, twining in and out of the ball of their bodies

— a mass of writhing reptiles enjoying the warm May sunshine. I loathe snakes with a passion that borders on obsession, and I ran from the scene in a complete panic. Once I had calmed down, I wondered how they had gotten there. I was sure there weren't supposed to be any snakes in Canada. That's one of the reasons I had come to Canada instead of going to Malaya or the Gold Coast of Africa. I knew they had snakes and I wouldn't go anywhere near those places.

Later, old Thomas Big-Blood told me not to worry, that what I had seen were only garter snakes and they were not poisonous. They were common in that part of the country and congregated late each autumn to hibernate for the winter. What I had witnessed were the snakes waking up with the mild spring weather.

At the end of May, I baled the fur, closed up my books and the post and returned to Minaki. It was rather sad to leave One Man Lake, knowing that I would not return. I had enjoyed my two winters' tenure and had gotten on well with the native people.

9

GRASSY NARROWS: 1935-36

After spending a few days with Mr Yelland winding up the affairs of the outpost, I caught the train to Winnipeg to find out what the future held for me. I hoped that this time I would be given a posting in the Arctic. When I was ushered into the fur trade commissioner's office, he came straight to the point.

'Ross,' he said, 'you will spend this coming summer assisting Mr Yelland again. Take a couple of weeks off in September and get married to that nice girl of yours. Then I am sending you to take charge of Grassy Narrows.'

I was appalled. This didn't fit into my scheme of things at all. 'But sir, my apprenticeship will be finished shortly and I am due six months' furlough, with my return fare paid to Scotland.'

He looked at me. 'You can forget about that just now. Anyway, six months is far too long. At the end of three months, you will be more than glad to come back to Canada. Believe me, I know.' I didn't know what to say. He shuffled some papers on his desk, and added, 'Now, you go to Grassy Narrows and in two years' time, that's 1937, you can take your three months' vacation.'

'But Grassy Narrows! I've been there already and it's not a good place to bring a new bride. The buildings are old and the furniture is awful. Haven't you any other posts I can go to?'

I could see that he wasn't too pleased. 'Now look, Ross. All staff movements have been arranged and you are scheduled to go to Grassy Narrows. Do you want it or not?'

Well, I had said my piece and one didn't argue with the fur trade commissioner. In 1935, a secure job wasn't something to be treated lightly. Reluctantly, I agreed to go but I cringed at the thought of Bea's face when she had a look at the almost primitive quarters that would be her first home.

'Good,' said Mr Parsons. 'That's settled. You will get good experience being in charge of Grassy Narrows and I guarantee you will not stay there longer than two years. You can take your holidays to the Old Country starting at the end of June, 1937. When you return, we will have a new posting for you.'

That evening, rather glumly, I broke the news to Bea. She took it much more calmly than I had expected. 'It's all right, honey. We'll make out. Anyway, we can't afford to go to Britain just now. If we save all our money for the next two years, we can have a super time on our honeymoon.'

I returned to Minaki and soon was busy getting things ready for the summer season. Bert McNaughton arrived again from Winnipeg to work with me in the store. At the end of June, schools closed for the summer holidays and Bea came down to Holst Point. Skipper Holst wanted to hear all about our plans and treated Bea as if she were his own daughter. Summer passed and we returned to Winnipeg for our wedding which was set for 25 September.

On the morning of 23 September, Marian Ross, Mr Parson's secretary, called me on the telephone. 'Can you come down to the office right away? Mr Parsons wants to see you immediately.' She sounded so urgent that I called a taxi and hurried down to Hudson's Bay House.

As I walked into his office, Mr Parsons exclaimed, 'By God, Ross, you were right. Grassy Narrows is a mess. The place has been allowed to go to rack and ruin. You simply cannot take your new wife to the post in that condition.' Calling Marian into his office, he said, 'Miss Ross, can you find anyone around — a post manager or someone whom I can send into Grassy Narrows tonight.' While Marian hurried to do his bidding, Mr Parsons told me that he had just come back from an inspection trip to Red Lake. While flying south from Red Lake to Kenora, the pilot pointed out Grassy Narrows below. 'Grassy Narrows,' Parsons said. 'I have a new manager going in there. Let's go down and have a look at it.' The result was my summons to his office.

'You'll certainly need some new furniture. What shall we send in? A new chesterfield and chair, a new stove — that old thing will burn the house down. Some new linoleum for the floor. How about that? What else do you think you will need?' I told him that we were shipping in Bea's own bedroom suite. 'Then you won't be needing new beds. Anything else?' I thought for several seconds and suggested a kitchen cabinet and perhaps, a carpet for the floor. Mr Parsons jotted them down on his list. I was feeling better by the minute. At least Bea wouldn't be living in complete squalor. 'No sir,' I said. 'That should do us just now. But I'm afraid that there are going to be a lot of repairs necessary for the house.' He had been so generous, I was almost afraid to bring it up.

'Can you do them yourself?' he asked.

'If I can hire a couple of Indians to help me, I think I can manage it, sir.'

Marian Ross returned with a young post manager in tow. James Boyd had just returned from his furlough in Scotland and was on his way west. 'Oh good,' said Mr Parsons. 'Boyd, I want you to do something for me. Take this list right over to the retail store, ask for the manager of the furniture department and tell him I want this order filled immediately. It is to be packed securely and shipped by express on tonight's train to Kenora. I realize that is not very much time, but if you have any trouble at the retail store, tell the manager to phone me.' Jimmy looked from the boss to me, wondering just what was going on. I was absolutely delighted at this turn of events.

'Now Boyd, I want you to go down to Kenora on the same train. When you get there, charter an aircraft, fly the furniture into Grassy Narrows and have it all set up when Mr and Mrs Ross arrive in a few days' time.' The young post manager took the list and hurried out to carry out his orders. Poor Jimmy Boyd. I'm sure he had other more interesting plans for the evening but away he went to do the shopping. Mr Parsons turned to me. 'Ross, as soon as you get to Grassy Narrows and settled in, I want you to make out a list of all necessary repairs, with estimates of the cost and send them to me for my okay.' I agreed to do this and thanked him for his generosity.

On 25 September 1935, Beatrice Vivian Dingle and Hugh Mackay Ross were married by the Reverend Dr A. E. Kerr in St. Augustine Church in Winnipeg. As we walked up the aisle after the ceremony, I noticed Mr Parsons sitting at the back of the church. Among our wedding gifts was a beautiful sterling silver tray inscribed:

Presented to Mr. and Mrs. H. M. Ross
by the Fur Trade Commissioner,
Hudson's Bay Company, on the occasion of their marriage,
September 25th, 1935.

Following a small reception at the home of Bea's parents, we caught the evening train for Minaki. It was already dark when we got off the train at the far end of the platform. The station was deserted except for Roy Grellier who came to take us to his house where we were to spend the night. At the front door of his home, he ushered us in ahead of him. Someone yelled, 'Surprise, surprise' as the lights went on. Everyone in town was gathered there to welcome us.

Bert McNaughton acted as master of ceremonies and after the usual toasts were offered, he presented us with a number of gifts on behalf of the community, including an Aladdin lamp, a Coleman gasoline-operated iron, and a large dry cell flashlight. Unorthodox perhaps, but we made good use of them in the days that followed. Mrs Grellier had prepared a sumptuous feast for the occasion and gave Bea recipes of several dishes that she knew I liked. When we declared that we were tired and wished to get some sleep, several of my chums escorted us to the bedroom with all kinds of advice to me on how to conduct myself. I was used to Hayward's ribald sense of humour, but poor Bea's face was burning.

Madame Grellier outdid herself the next morning, serving us breakfast in bed. We had quite a send-off when the Stinson float plane from Kenora arrived to pick us up. As we taxied across the water, there was Skipper Holst standing in front of the flag-pole at the point. He dipped the flag in salute as we raced over the water and then climbed into the blue sky en route to our life at Grassy Narrows.

As we flew northeast over the lake-studded bush, the pilot, Stan Wagner, told me that his company was flying from Kenora to Red Lake almost daily and that his route passed directly over Grassy Narrows. They would bring in our mail every two weeks and would appreciate any freighting business that we could turn their way. This proved to be a good arrangement for us. We received mail regularly and a steady supply of fresh meat and vegetables. During the next two years, Stan Wagner and another pilot, Davy Glenn, became regular visitors to our island. They were both accommodating and never failed in their efforts to obtain any items of a personal nature that we required.

John Patience and Jimmy Boyd were waiting to meet us when the plane pulled up on the beach at Grassy Narrows. As Stan quickly unloaded our luggage, he said, 'Sorry folks, I can't stay long this trip. I have another flight to make to Red Lake today.' Jimmy climbed aboard with his suitcase and as Stan pushed the aircraft off the beach with his paddle, he shouted, 'I'll be back in three or four days to pick you up, Mr Patience.' We watched the plane take off the water safely and then walked up the path to the house.

We went in by the side door that led into the kitchen. There was our brand new stove, all assembled and ready to go. It was a beautiful stove, cream enamel with chromium trim. It had a high-rise oven at the back and a copper, hot-water reservoir at one side. Against the other wall of the kitchen was the new cabinet; there were compartments for groceries, drawers for cutlery and glass-fronted shelves for dishes on top.

In the living-room, there was a fine new Kroehler chesterfield and armchair. I glanced quickly at Bea to see how she was reacting to all this. As our eyes met, she smiled and nodded her head, indicating that she was pleased. So far, so good, I thought. Then I noticed that the old linoleum was still on the floor, still worn bare down the centre where Donald Murchison had paced back and forth for so many years. John saw me looking at it and before I could say anything, he quickly said, 'I'll explain about the linoleum in a few minutes.'

As I started to walk into the main bedroom, he yelled a warning. 'No! Don't go in there. Let me go first.' Flipping back the floor covering, he showed me a large gaping hole in the wooden floor. Apparently there had been an old cellar, of which I knew nothing, underneath the floorboards. The cellar had filled with water and the floor planks had rotted and disintegrated. In order to reach the bed, John explained, we had to go carefully around both walls and not directly over the floor. 'I think you had better use the office bedroom until you get this fixed up,' he advised us.

The office safe, which usually stood behind the door in the bedroom, had fallen through the floorboards and was standing on the earth below. The door of the safe could be opened only with great difficulty. It just cleared the floorboards.

John Patience looked at us sheepishly and said, 'I'm afraid there's more.' There was a rotten piece of flooring about three feet square beside the living-room window; it was covered by the table. Thoroughly disgusted, I decided to go outside to cool off. But when I yanked the front door open, the handle came off in my hand and the door stayed firmly shut. I tried it again, but it wouldn't budge. John explained that with the continuous sinking of the logs, he had tried to keep the door open by cutting wedges off the top and bottom of the door but had finally gotten fed up and simply used the kitchen entrance.

After supper, Bea and I wandered around the island. The small grass plot in front of the house was immaculate but the balance of the clearing was in terrible shape. The grass hadn't been cut all summer. Weeds, grass and thistles stood three feet high. A small beaten-down path led from the house through the long grass to the outhouse. At the far end of the island, we stopped and sat down on the rocks. I looked at Bea. She looked at me. Then we both burst out laughing. 'A hell of a mess, isn't it?' I said. 'Do you think you can stand it?'

'Oh sure,' she replied. 'It certainly can't get any worse and by next summer, we'll have it all straightened away.' She started to giggle and said, 'Can't you just imagine the look on my father's face if he saw this place?' As we walked slowly back to the house, I wondered if she knew just how much her words meant to me.

Next morning, John and I started in on the change of management inventory. Fortunately, he had already brought in his winter supplies in anticipation of the change-over. There were many interruptions, of course. When the Indians heard that I had returned, they all came over to greet me and meet my new wife. Each one came up, solemnly shook hands with us and said, 'Bojo, bojo' meaning 'Hello, hello.'

John was on pins and needles to get to his new posting at Fort Hope. Every time an airplane passed overhead, he dropped everything, grabbed his suitcase and overcoat, shouted 'Good bye', and raced down to the beach. When it just kept on going, he sadly shook his head, trudged slowly up the path to the house, deposited his suitcase once again by the kitchen door and resumed working. Eventually the plane did come and John Patience left. Poor John. In his efforts to turn in a good profit to the Company, he had gone overboard. To keep his expenses down, he had neglected the day-to-day repairs which should always have been done. They had piled up into the present sorry mess. I never saw him again. In a letter he wrote to me a few months later from his new post in Fort Hope, he proudly stated, 'I am in charge of 300 fur-bearing natives.' Much later, I heard that he had married the daughter of Johnny Yes-No, a free trader at Fort Hope. He quit the Company and with the backing of his father-in-law, he opened a store of his own at Armstrong.

The following Sunday, Bea and I had a visit from three fire rangers who were stationed about four miles south of us at the other end of the portage leading from Grassy Narrows Lake to Delaney Lake. They told us the story of the immaculate lawn in front of the house. On his furlough to Scotland, John Patience had become enamoured of the game of golf. On his return, he cut the grass and turned the front lawn into a nine-hole putting green with tin cans sunk into the ground for holes. He bought a small, second-hand lawnmower and religiously cut the grass every second day, until it was like a bowling green. When the fire rangers visited him, John immediately asked, 'Care for a game of golf, gentlemen?' If they agreed, he ran into the house, donned his plus fours and golf shoes and reappeared with a bunch of putters and golf balls. And they played a round of nine-hole putting.

Bea and I made good use of the putting green. Once spring came we bought an outdoor badminton set, rigged up the net and spent many hours at the game. Bea was an expert player and beat me unmercifully.

The month of October was busy. I hired my old friends, Michell Keesik and John Loon, to cut the long grass with scythes. They raked it into heaps and let it dry out; then on the first calm, windless day, we set fire to the piles, watching carefully that the fire did not spread. I sent six men down to Jones Station with one of the freight canoes to bring back our personal baggage and furniture. There was lots of spare lumber upstairs in the store attic, and with it, I laid a temporary floor over the rotten bit in the main bedroom. I had visions of getting up in the middle of the night, forgetting about it and falling through.

When our things arrived at the post, we set up Bea's bedroom suite and unpacked our wedding gifts, some of which we hadn't seen yet. Among the baggage was a washing-machine which I had purchased without Bea's knowledge. I suppose it would qualify as a curiosity today, but in 1935 it was the latest thing and sure beat washing clothes by hand. The machine was a round, wooden tub mounted on four legs. The top lifted up on hinges. Inside was a four-pinned dolly, rotated by a series of wheels and gears on top of the lid. By pumping a handle back and forth, the wheels and gears agitated the dollies and did a fair job of the wash.

Wash-day was a serious business. The evening before, I filled up the forty-five gallon barrel which stood beside the kitchen stove. This water had to be carried up the hill from the lake, two pails at a time. First thing in the morning I lit the fire and placed a large copper boiler containing about ten gallons of water on top of the stove. The reservoir was also filled. When the water was hot, Bea went ahead with her laundry. Whenever she required more hot water or the barrel needed refilling, she gave me a shout and it was back down the hill with my two pails. I often marvelled at the way she cheerfully went about these arduous tasks that were completely new to her.

We scrubbed all the interior ceilings and walls and painted them with Alabastine — a forerunner, I think, of emulsion paints. It came in powder form in five-pound packs in various colours. We mixed it with water and then applied it. Three coats were needed to do a satisfactory job on the old canoe-enamel paint-

work. We unpacked our china and silverware, giving Mr Parsons'
tray a place of honour. Then, while Bea hung curtains she had
made in Winnipeg at the windows, I put up a few pictures and
sketches we had bought. We sat back, looked around and smil-
ingly realized we were home.

Another of my purchases was a new battery pack for the
radio. The reception was excellent at Grassy Narrows; we drew up
a timetable of our favourite programs and pinned it on the wall
over the set.

Bea was a fine cook and, despite the fact that she had never
used one before, soon mastered the intricacies of the wood stove.
She only had one problem with it. I came in one morning to find
her in tears, looking down at a mess of blackened goo on the
bottom of the oven. As I comforted her and cleaned it up, she
tearfully explained that she was going to surprise me with a
custard pie, but that half the filling had spilled over the edge of the
crust because the 'blankety blank' stove was tilted, because the
'blankety blank' floor was sloping to one side like a drunk after a
party. Try as we might, we couldn't lift the stove to put a wedge
underneath, so Bea solved the problem by placing the pie crust on
the rack first and then slowly adding the filling. Nevertheless, for
the next few months, all her pies were lopsided.

*   *   *

In October the Indians began preparing for their sojourn at
the trapping grounds. They came over to the store to ask how
much debt I was going to give them. 'Debt' was the general term in
the North applied to any merchandise advanced on credit to a
trapper against his hunt. As the pre-Christmas season is usually
the best time for catching fur, the fall debt is usually fairly large. If
this fall debt was paid at Christmas, then a smaller spring debt
was advanced. Again, if the spring debt was paid, a small debt was
given against the muskrat and beaver trapping season in April
and May. It was the trapper's responsibility to pay his debt in full
when he returned with his fur, thus keeping his credit rating good
so that he could always come back for a further advance.

On examining the customers' records, which were reports of

Pilot Davy Glenn with the mail plane, a Stinson Detroiter, at Grassy Narrows, autumn, 1935.

each Indian's trading, year by year, at the post, I was astonished to find that each page was headed by such terms as 'scoundrel', 'rogue', 'rascal', 'thief', or 'liar'. John Patience obviously didn't have a high opinion of the Grassy Narrows trappers. The list of proposed debt which he had submitted to District Office for authorization was much more encouraging. I discussed his record with each trapper when he came to the store and decided on the amount to be advanced. In due course, all the good trappers left for their traplines; there were only a few pot-hunters who stayed around the post. On the whole, they weren't very good trappers; we only allowed them debt up to $5.00 at any one time. In order to repay their debt, they went into the bush and returned with one mink, fox, or otter pelt.

John Loon and Michell Keesik came under the pot-hunter category, but rather than being trappers they were good workmen, and I was able to give them enough casual work to keep them in supplies.

Late in October, Stan Wagner arrived with the mail.

'This could be my last trip until freeze-up,' he said. 'If the weather continues mild, I could get in another trip, but don't count on it.' He then explained, 'We can't land on the lake until there are nine inches of good, blue ice.' He pointed to a long bay which stretched from the island westward. 'That would make a good landing strip,' he said. 'You will have to measure the ice carefully and pay special attention to the centre part where the river current flows past the bay. There has to be a minimum of nine inches of clear, blue ice the whole length of the runway before we can land. When you are sure that is the case, mark out the runway with spruce trees.' Once Stan was assured that we understood, he flew off.

The lake froze over in early November and each day I checked the ice, but the temperature stayed mild and I couldn't get that nine inches of blue ice. The snow kept falling and there was a lot of slush ice. It was 15 December before I could really say that I had a sufficient depth of ice for the plane to land. Michell, John Loon and I cut a bunch of small spruce trees and marked out the sides of the runway. Daily, Bea and I waited and although we heard planes flying overhead almost every day, none of them landed at Grassy Narrows.

It soon became clear that we weren't going to receive any mail or presents in time for Christmas. It was annoying for me, but I was heartsick for Bea as I checked our supplies to see what we could substitute for a Christmas dinner. Bea was wonderful. She had the capacity to disregard the things she couldn't do anything about, and to make the best of our assets. Her sense of fun was contagious, so we went ahead with our holiday preparations anyway.

After long and careful deliberation, we selected our Christmas tree. This wasn't your casual meandering down to a corner lot to choose one of hundreds tied up with string. In November we had taken an inspection trip of our own, looking each tree over and taking note of its position in the woods. Eventually we narrowed down our selection, made our choice and marked it with a ribbon Bea took from her hair. We also drew up a map, because a tree covered with snow looks very different without it. Seventy-five steps from the birch tree, then thirty-three steps left and fourteen steps right. There it was, still wearing Bea's bright

Hugh and Beatrice Ross carrying water and waiting for the nine inches of clear blue ice required for the landing of the mail plane.

red ribbon for identification. I cut it down and we carried it home in triumph.

We were busy in the store the week before Christmas when the Indians all returned from their trapping grounds. The season had been good and they all had fairly large catches. They were able to pay off their debts and still have enough money to trade. Then they left to visit their children at the residential school in McIntosh.

I arrived back at the house to find that Bea had decorated it with spruce boughs and ribbons and she had even made some icicles for the tree. She'd cut them out of cardboard and wrapped them in silver and gold paper — the wrappings on our wedding gifts. During the evening, as we listened to the radio, we made chains from the paper, painted pine cones, and hung up a star that I had carved from a bit of balsam. I think that tree was the prettiest we ever had.

Our Christmas dinner wasn't what I had planned at all. Usually the Company supplied a complete turkey dinner, right down to the plum pudding, but because the plane had not arrived, we sat down to a large piece of bologna, stuck with cloves and decorated with slices of pineapple. Bea roasted it in the oven and baked some potatoes. For dessert, we had canned peaches with Carnation milk and a delicious Christmas cake that Bea had baked in October.

We lit the candles, opened a bottle of wine we had saved and thus, spent our first Christmas together in our own home.

On 11 January, the first winter plane finally arrived; the pilot was most apologetic. 'I'm sorry we couldn't get here before Christmas, Mr Ross. We had so many charters to Red Lake we just didn't have time to stop here with a part load,' he explained. Joyfully, we lugged our supplies up to the house. There was more than two months' mail, newspapers, gifts from family and friends and, of course, our Christmas dinner. We planned to spend a long evening, reading letters and opening the gifts. The dinner could wait for another day.

Just as we were comfortably settled, there was a knock on the door. Standing outside were three young white men, looking very tired. 'Could you put us up for the night?' one asked. We assured them that they were most welcome and Bea went to prepare a meal. As they wearily removed their coats and had a cup of tea, they told us their story. They lived in Kenora and had been out of work for some time. So the previous fall, they decided to go north for the winter to try their hand at trapping. They had been outfitted by a Mr Silverman, a fur buyer in Kenora, who had chartered a plane in October and had them flown to a lake about forty miles northeast of Grassy Narrows. Their intention was to live in the cabin and trap until the following spring when the plane was scheduled to return to pick them up.

By the end of December, however, they had had enough of the bush and decided to pack it in and walk out to Kenora. It was my guess that, with the three of them cooped up together, they had come down with a bad case of 'cabin fever'. After talking it over for several days, they went out and picked up their traps and cached them safely. For two days, they travelled south to the English River and then following the river west, walked until they hit our post. They were hungry for conversation. We were the first people that they had encountered since they left Kenora in

October. The poor fellows went on and on. It was in the wee, small hours of the morning before we got them bedded down in their blankets on the living room floor and retired to the quiet of our bedroom. It was too late and we were too sleepy to dig into our long awaited mail.

After breakfast, they sold me some of their skins so that they had some cash in their pockets. The balance of their catch had to be taken to Kenora to repay Mr Silverman. They offered to pay for their meals, but I refused, explaining that it was the policy of the Hudson's Bay Company to always extend hospitality to any travellers in the North.

They planned to head south, across country straight to Kenora. Spreading their map on the counter, I pointed out the route south to Jones Station and explained that there was a good dog-team trail all the way there. 'You might be able to catch a freight train from Jones to Redditt, which is about ten miles west. There's a road from Redditt south to Kenora and you might be lucky and pick up a ride. Even if you have to walk the track to Redditt, it's much safer than trying to cut through the bush. There's no marked trail south of Jones and you might get lost.' As we helped them pack up their gear, they whispered to each other and then placed a bundle of ermine skins in Bea's hands. 'We'd like you to have these, Ma'am. You and Mr Ross have been very kind. But the thing we missed most was the sound of a lady's voice, and we very much appreciate all your trouble.'

We watched them go south across the lake until they hit the trail and then we raced each other to the house to open our mail. That evening we had our real Christmas dinner: roast turkey, cranberry sauce and candied yams. Even walnuts.

Bea took most things in her stride but the previous fall, with the advent of snow, we had the usual influx of field mice coming in from under the floor, and she wasn't amused. There was no trouble in the store or the two warehouses, as they were adequately protected against mice. Moreover, the small tracks of ermine in the snow attested to the fact that any mice trying to get into these buildings would have little chance of survival; ermine count mice as one of their favourite foods. It was a different matter in the house, however, and trapping operations had to be put into effect immediately. We managed to get rid of most of them but we could still hear them scurrying along in the spaces between the logs and the wainscoting at night. One morning, while sleepily going to wash my face in the basin, I reached up for the soap in the dish and discovered a mouse calmly sitting there eating the soap. That did it! We would have to get either a cat or a small dog. Both Bea and I disliked cats, so it would have to be a dog.

I wrote to a pet shop in Winnipeg, enclosing $10.00, and asked them to send me a small dog — any breed, provided he could catch mice. On the next plane, ensconced in a wooden box that normally held twenty-five pounds of prunes, was a small, black and white, smooth-haired fox terrier. He was dressed in a garment made by cutting holes in a woollen sock, to protect him from the cold. The mechanics in Kenora had looked after him and fed him while he was waiting to catch the plane. We promptly named him Peter, for absolutely no good reason. That night we lined a basket for him at the foot of the bed but he insisted on trying to leap into bed to sleep with us. When he was firmly rejected, he whined piteously for some time before deciding that we meant business and finally went to sleep.

During the night, we were awakened by a loud disturbance. Peter jumped up on the bed, his little tail wagging furiously, holding a mouse between his jaws. He deposited the mouse on the pillow beside me and looked at us expectantly. While I disposed of the creature, Bea praised him and told him what a good boy he was. The matter was settled. From then on, Peter slept at the bottom of our bed, curled up under the comforter. Peter was a great mouser, and in no time he had cleaned the pests out. The following spring, he had a wonderful time mouse-hunting out of doors. After cleaning out the house, he started on those which nested in the grass near the building. Then he looked for further game and discovered that they went underground. Often, all we could see of the wee dog was the tip of his tail waving wildly as he dug right down until he reached the nest.

It seemed to me that Bea had adjusted beautifully to life in the bush. When I asked her about it, she agreed that she was enjoying it very much. 'But . . .' She stopped and looked at me.

'Come on, honey, but what?'

'Well, I learned how to manage the stove, and Peter has taken care of all the mice. I've even become used to taking a bath in the round zinc bathtub in front of the wood stove, but . . .' She stopped again, then blurted out, 'I hate having to go outside in all kinds of weather to use the biffy.'

She was right of course. It is one of the curses of life in the North to have to walk fifty yards to the outhouse when it is twenty degrees below zero and then to have to sweep away an inch of rime frost before sitting down on the ice-cold seat.

The next order I placed was for a chemical toilet. I built a partition in a corner of the bedroom and, despite her questions, I didn't tell Bea what it was for. When it arrived and I had the toilet installed, Bea almost wept with delight.

The chemical toilet was a simple contraption. It was made of sheet iron with a wooden seat and lid. Inside was a ten-gallon pail, into which I poured a measured amount of chemical, and there it was — an inside toilet. The whole thing was supposed to be connected by pipes to an outside vent. I solved this problem by hooking it up to the stove pipe which wound its way from the kitchen, through the bedroom and finally, up to the attic. What a luxury! No more climbing out of a warm bed, dressing in heavy clothes, three pairs of socks and moccasins, and trudging through the snow in the freezing cold.

By mid-January, all the trappers were outfitted and sent off again. The weather turned colder and the temperature didn't rise above -20 F at mid-day. The nights were lovely; deathly quiet with not a breath of wind. We spent hours looking out of the window at the aurora borealis and the myriad stars.

The pine and spruce trees on the nearby islands stood out in a jagged pattern, sharply etched against the sky. The only movement was the smoke which rose in straight, thin, white columns from the chimneys on the reserve. Occasionally, the ice exploded with loud booms as the increasing pressure forced the ice to crack into ridges which spread for miles along the surface of the ice. Inside the house, we were sometimes disturbed by loud sharp cracks in the log walls. These alarmed Bea until I explained that it was just the frost in the logs expanding.

Business was slack, so I set about drawing up my estimates for the required repairs. With the exception of the three holes in the floor, I found that the rest of the planks were in good shape. All the log stringers under the floor had to be replaced, however. Some were rotten and only by replacing them all could the slopes in the floor be fixed. The front door still didn't close properly and when I examined it, I discovered that the bottom two logs in the wall of the house were rotten too. Only the interior lining of tongue and groove board was preventing the logs from sagging further. Rather than take any chances, I decided that the bottom three tiers would have to be replaced all around.

It was the custom in the North at that time to bank the outside of the house with earth. This was done every fall to keep out the frost. Normally, before this banking was done, a sheet of tarpaper was placed against the logs to prevent any damp from attacking the logs through the earth. The protective lining hadn't been used at Grassy Narrows, nor had the banking been removed each spring; this explained the deterioration.

It was a Company regulation that all stove pipes were to be cleaned out thoroughly once a month, checked, and any necessary replacements made. This was essential to prevent fire. There was almost no hope of saving a building in the North, once it caught fire.

On a trip to the attic in October, I had noticed a large tarpaulin spread out on the floor. It was directly under a leak in the roof and directly above the place where John Patience had his bed in the room below. Instead of fixing the leak as soon as he discovered it, John used the tarp as a temporary measure; then he promptly forgot about it. So now I had to fix the roof too. When all the repairs were completed, I would have to replaster and finish all the outside walls of the building. I sometimes thought it would have been simpler just to build a new house.

I drew up my report, complete with estimates of costs, and sent it in to District Office, adding that I thought I would be able to make the repairs with the assistance of two or three of the Indians. I planned to start the work right after break-up. In due course, permission was granted. The letter ended with the usual injunction, 'In carrying out these repairs, you will take every precaution to keep expenditures as low as possible.'

*   *   *

In March, the Reverend Canon Maurice Sanderson paid us a visit on his regular trip to parishioners around the country. He was a remarkable man and one of the few really good men I have ever met. A Cree Indian, born and brought up around Moose Factory, he was now in charge of the Anglican Church missions for nearly all the reserves in Northwest Ontario. His visits to his far-flung parishioners kept him travelling, by canoe in summer and dog-team in winter. He was widely known throughout the area and respected by everyone with whom he came in contact. His home was in Kenora where he lived with his family. One of his sons was an outstanding player on the old Kenora Thistles hockey team.

The following morning, Roderick Land — whose Indian name was Atanamagan — came over to pick up the Canon. Roderick was a real old-time Indian. Every Sunday morning, as a local deacon, he conducted religious services in the reserve's council house. He was as honest as the day is long. Although too old to trap, he lived well, as he was a good hunter and fisherman. His two sons, Robert and James, were first-class hunters like their father. Roderick was the only Indian I knew who owned a birch-bark canoe. It was a small, twelve-foot craft; he had built it himself and he paddled it all over the lake. I tried paddling it once, but quickly gave up. You really had to keep your tongue in the middle of your mouth; otherwise the canoe would capsize.

Roderick and Canon Sanderson left for the reserve right away and I didn't see them again until dinner time that evening. The Canon was practical as well as religious and had spent the first day visiting all the old people on the reserve. After dinner, he presented me with a long list of things he wanted for some of the elderly. The list covered everything from flannelette blankets and woollen stockings to flour, lard, baking powder and tobacco. He believed in looking after the body as well as the soul.

'Just make out your counterslips under the individual names and charge them to the Department of Indian Affairs, Kenora,' he said. 'I'll sign the bills when they are ready. He then showed me a letter from Captain Frank Edwards, the Indian agent in Kenora, authorizing these purchases. In those 'good, old days', Treaty Indians did not receive old age pensions and the monthly ration they were issued from the Department of Indian Affairs did not cover all their needs. Canon Sanderson always saw to it that they got the things they required to make life more pleasant. The following day, he conducted religious services, which were attended by all the Anglicans on the reserve. Where necessary, he performed marriages and he baptized any babies that had been born since his last visit.

After dinner that evening, we got to discussing the Ojibway language. 'You speak the language quite well — for a white man,' he said. 'But there are some rules which you should know about in order to speak it perfectly. I have a book at home that I'll send to you when I get back to Kenora.' Next morning, he left by dog-team for the railway track.

When the book arrived, it was a grammar and dictionary of the Ojibway language prepared by Father Chrysostom Verwyst, for use by the missionaries. It was a mine of information and I kept it for more than a year before I returned the book to Canon Sanderson. My long-felt suspicions were confirmed. Ojibway was not a simple, barbaric language. I had been using it in its simplest form and the Indians understood me. They, in turn, replied in the same simple form, so that I could understand them. But like the French, Latin and Greek languages, there were grammatical structures. There were also suffix endings for diminutives and for distinguishing good or bad. Short prefixes could change the meaning of a noun. It was confusing at first, but gradually the use of the rules became clearer. I tried my new vocabulary on my good friends, Michell Keesik and John Loon. Although they sometimes laughed at my attempts, they helped immensely and corrected me whenever I made a mistake.

One tense I could not master was the subjunctive. The Indian never says 'I will do something tomorrow'. He can't be sure if he will be alive tomorrow. So he uses the subjunctive and says

'Maybe I will do this tomorrow.' While, in time, my vocabulary improved greatly and I became quite fluent in Ojibway, I never did master the subjunctive.

Another strange thing was that the letter 'R' was seldom used. The Indians always referred to Mary Murchison as 'Many Munchison'. They had great difficulty with my name and seldom, if ever, addressed me as Mr Ross. In most cases I was the *ogema* or boss.

Nor were there any swear words. Parts of the body were simply parts of the body. If an Indian was angry, he might exclaim *Machi Manito* — bad spirit. Or he might refer to someone as *cocosh* — pig. But if he was really angry and he wanted to swear, the Indian had to revert to speaking English.

I noticed that the Indians never referred to themselves as Ojibway. They were either *Anishinapiwok,* meaning Indian, or, as they preferred to call themselves, the *Ininaywok* — the people.

I have always liked the Indians and, in the many years I was closely associated with them, I got on well. I found that, unless they were in close contact with white people, they were utterly dependable and their word could be relied on. In the bush they were a class unto themselves. They could live where a white man would perish. If one man shot a moose, he shared it with everyone else. He knew that sometime it would be his turn to be on the receiving end. Although all the men were not first-class trappers, they could always catch a small amount of fur to trade for their immediate necessities, and they were adept at fishing and hunting. If ammunition was scarce, they knew how to set snares and deadfalls.

In the old days, young boys always went along to the trapping grounds with their parents and were taught, at an early age, the many skills required to survive in the bush. Now, all the children — boys and girls — were taken by the missionaries to residential schools. There they were taught the three 'R's' and other white man's skills. At the age of seventeen or eighteen, they returned to the reserve, totally ignorant of how to make a living by trapping or hunting. Sometimes the error was compounded by marriages encouraged by the schools. The results were often too sad to contemplate.

Years later, when family allowances were paid to all parents, including Treaty Indians, schools were built on the reserves. In order for the mother to collect this money, the children had to attend the school. So the mother stayed home to look after her children, while the father went alone to his trapping ground. But he made frequent trips back to visit his family and in doing so, reduced the amount of time he spent making the rounds of his traplines. Thus his income and standard of living slowly diminished.

To my mind, these two actions led to the breakdown of the nomadic and self-sufficient life of the Indian people. Young people, taught in the white man's schools, drifted to towns and cities, hoping to get the jobs that the schools had prepared them for. They didn't get those jobs, and any jobs they did get were usually of the most menial and temporary nature.

*   *   *

In April, the weather became milder. Snow melted on the roof and long icicles dripped from the eaves. There was a balmy feeling in the air. The ice started to candle and break away at the shoreline. Crows appeared and even the birds seemed to chirp more cheerfully. Although we were situated on an island, we weren't cut off from the reserve for too many days. Early in the morning, the ice tightened up with the frost and the Indians came scooting across it before the temperature warmed up. They sat on little sleighs and pushed themselves rapidly forward with two sticks. They seemed to be able to pick out the good and bad spots on the ice and always made it safely.

Bea had never seen a river breaking up and we spent hours sitting on the rocks in the warming sun, watching the huge pans of ice drifting in the wind and crashing up against the rocks; there they hung until they disintegrated in the warm sun.

The winter trapping season closed officially at the end of February, and by early March the Indians were all back on the reserve. The hunt had been reasonably good and in addition to doing a brisk trade, I had collected almost 100 per cent of all advances. During the interim period, until the muskrat season

Ojibway trappers hauling firewood during the slow season at Grassy Narrows, March 1936.

opened, I set the Indians to work cutting my next winter's supply of firewood. They went a few miles up the river to get beyond the boundaries of the reserve, cut a supply of jackpine, sawed it into four-foot lengths, and piled it by the shore to be ferried to the post by canoe after open water. There was little birch in this part of the country, so jackpine had to be used instead. After it had been seasoned over the summer months, this wood threw a good heat, but it was full of creosote and tended to foul the stove-pipes quickly. So we made sure that the pipes were cleaned when the winter heater was in use. A small quantity of poplar wood was also sawn up. It made an excellent fuel for the cookstove. When split and dried, it burned with a quick, hot flame and left almost no ash.

While the other men were cutting firewood, John Loon and Michell Keesik were busy knocking down an old log house which I had purchased on the reserve. The logs were hauled across to the island by dog-team and gave me a good supply of well-seasoned, square timbers which I required for repairing the house. They were long enough to do both ends of the house and the front. But I needed three extra long logs to go the whole length of the back of the house. John and Michell went out to cut them, as well as the logs I needed for the stringers.

There was no flag-pole at the post and I thought it was time we had one, so I asked them to get a long, straight jackpine and three good-sized ten-foot logs for supports. It was an easy job to haul the logs over the ice, now that the snow was gone. All the logs had to be peeled and squared and, working with John and Michell, I had my first lesson in the use of a broadaxe and chalk line. The jackpine for the flag-pole was also peeled and set on trestles to dry out straight and true.

At long last we were all set to start fixing up the house. We nailed two-by-fours at intervals vertically on the outside walls, to keep the logs in position while we jacked up the house. A small hole was dug at each corner and the rotten bottom logs pulled out carefully. Then we placed a flat stone at the bottom of the hole and on top of the stone, a screw-jack, which we used in our fur-baling press. Slowly the jack was screwed up until the whole corner was lifted up a few inches. Then a crib of firewood logs was put under it. The other three corners were done in the same way, one after the other. By jacking up each corner in sequence, a few inches at a time, we gradually raised the house enough to extract the three rotten logs. Next we inserted the new stringers under the floor alongside the old ones. Fortunately, it was a floating floor, not attached to the side walls, so this part of the job wasn't too difficult. We installed the three bottom logs all round and let the house back down onto its new foundation.

Next we tackled the cellar. The water was bailed out by the pailful via the bedroom window and the water hole filled up with barrow loads of earth and rock. The rotten parts of the flooring were replaced with sound lumber and then we were able to lay down our brand new linoleum on the now-level floor. I really felt that we should have had some sort of official ceremony over the linoleum, in remembrance of Donald Murchison, but Bea said we were too busy for such foolishness.

It had been a ticklish job and I was thankful when it was completed. John and Michell might not have been great trappers but they certainly knew how to handle tools. While this work was going on, Bea and I camped out in a tent. She took the disruption like a trooper and watched our efforts with great interest. Peter tended to get under our feet so she put on his lead and took him

Unidentified tourists in front of the Grassy Narrows dwelling house, prior to renovations in the spring, 1936.

away from the worksite. When we moved back into the house, she said, 'Thank goodness, now we'll be able to have pies that aren't all lopsided.' And that's the first thing she baked.

The roof was next on the agenda and John and Michell made short work of that. In no time, we had a brand new roof of red rubberoid securely nailed and cemented down, proof against any weather that might come.

All that remained now was the plastering between the logs. Since this was a slow job, I decided to do it myself in my spare time. The old plaster had to be cleaned from between the logs, then small shingle nails driven in about six inches apart to give the plaster a grip. I mixed up the plaster down at the beach, one barrow load at a time. I used three parts of sand to one part of lime, plus sufficient water to make a stiff paste. The barrow load was wheeled up to the house and the plaster applied with a mason's trowel, working it right into the cracks between the logs and smoothing it firmly and evenly on the outside. It took a week for the plaster to dry and cure thoroughly in the warm sunshine.

Then two coats of lime wash were applied. A small amount of laundry blueing was added to the mixture and this made the lime wash dry to a dazzling whiteness. The windows and the doors were painted in the standard Company colours: red for the doors and green for the trim. When it was all finished, Bea and I knew we had a home of which we could be proud.

Erecting the new flag-pole came next. The three ten-foot logs which Michell and John had cut first had to be squared. Although my broadaxe work was amateurish to begin with, it improved as I went along and the final result was quite passable. The butt end of the flag-pole was squared off and the whole pole painted white. One of the logs was sawn into two five-foot sections. The two ten-foot logs were bolted at right angles to the centre of one of them. The other section was inserted between them to act as a spreader. Three holes about a foot and a half apart were bored in each upright, and a corresponding three holes, in the base of the flag-pole.

The completed base then was eased gently into a five-foot deep by five-foot long hole which I had dug for the purpose. It was manoeuvred around until it was perfectly perpendicular and the hole was filled in and firmly tamped down. We inserted the butt of the flagpole between the two uprights and fitted a long, iron bolt through the hole. With the help of several Indians and a ladder, the pole was swung upright and the other two iron bolts inserted and bolted securely.

Our post was now a real Hudson's Bay post. Bea had the honour of hoisting the flag for the first time.

*   *   *

By the end of May, 1936, the muskrat and beaver season was over. I closed off my books for the year and packed all the furs on hand for shipment to London. I was quite pleased with the year-end results. District Office must have been pleased also, because in September, I received a raise in wages of $10.00 a month.

In early June, I had our firewood supply brought down the river to the island in freight canoes. The logs were carried up to the post and piled neatly in the yard to cure for the next winter. I had the poplar logs for the kitchen stove piled separately. Sawing these into stove lengths and splitting them was a job I reserved to keep me busy during the idle summer months.

Father Lemire at the newly built
Grassy Narrows chapel, 1936.

Rear view of the chapel, show-
ing the priests' living quarters.

Father Lemire, a priest from the settlement of McIntosh on the railway, came up and camped on the reserve with his assistant and helper, Little Brother Grandpré. They were building a chapel to serve the needs of the Indians of their faith. The Indians had cut and peeled the logs for the building and, when these were erected, the Father and his helper completed the inside carpentry work, which included a beautiful little altar.

Bea and I paddled over several times to watch them at their work. Both these men were excellent bridge players and we enjoyed the pleasure of their company on many evenings. The bridge battles were most stimulating after the endless games of cribbage which Bea and I played during the winter.

The Indians had all moved out of their winter houses and were camping in the open. The reserve was dotted with white tents and in the evenings, we could see their campfires burning and hear the endless throbbing of their drums as they indulged in their age-old pastime of gambling. There were many strange faces around. Strange to me, that is. They were members of the Grassy Narrows Band who had moved away from the reserve and were living at various points along the railway tracks. They had all returned to Grassy Narrows to collect their treaty money.

Treaty Day is the one big annual event in the life of the Indian. On this day, as prescribed in the treaty made between the Indian band and the Crown, each Indian — man, woman and child — is paid an annual sum of money. In the case of the Grassy Narrows Indians, this was $5.00 per head. In addition, each councillor got an added sum, as did the Chief; and they were fitted out with a blue serge suit of office. The jacket of the suit had brass buttons and a strip of gold braid on the sleeves to designate the rank of the wearer. This year, Treaty Day at Grassy Narrows was 3 July.

Towards the end of June, I had an official visit from the Chief and his councillors. 'Was the Company,' they asked, 'going to provide them with the usual treaty feast?' This was the first inkling I had of a treaty feast. When I found out that all I had to do was to supply them with a quantity of salt pork, a couple of sacks of flour and baking powder to make bannock, and sufficient tea to make up a good brew, I readily agreed. I told them that, as they had paid off their debts well the previous year, I would throw in a sack of onions for good measure. The Indians were delighted. They loved onions.

The next request was a little more delicate. Would I advance the head of each family the usual treaty debt? I rather demurred at this, especially as many of the visiting Indians were complete strangers to me. The Chief soon put my mind at rest. He explained that the treaty debt was a debt that an Indian always honoured and that the Chief would guarantee payment. Moreover, he said that the debt should not be more than half the payment received by the individual. He gave me a list of all the heads of families, together with the amount of money each would receive. Given these assurances, I quickly agreed to advance the necessary credit and I didn't lose a single dollar. After treaty payment had been completed, the councillors checked with me regularly until all outstanding accounts were paid in full.

In preparation for Treaty Day, I ordered a complete plane-

Treaty Days at Grassy Narrows, 1936. Canon Sanderson, Captain Frank Edwards and an unidentified doctor from the Department of Indian Affairs.

Tents of the treaty party, with the heads of family filing in to receive treaty payments in new one-dollar bills.

load of dry goods — mostly prints and ribbons, and lots of candy for the children. The Indians loved their children and no matter how little money they had, they would always buy some candy for them. For a week I was extremely busy in the store. Everybody was feeling happy and contented. They were all well fed and well dressed in preparation for the big day.

Treaty Day arrived. Early in the afternoon, we heard a volley of shots from the lookout party stationed at a point south of the post. The whole tribe made their way down to the shore. Soon the canoes carrying the treaty party swept into sight, with each canoe flying a Union Jack from the bow. They made straight for the beach in front of the band's council house. When they landed, they were greeted with a fusillade of shots from the rifles and shotguns held by every man.

Tents were quickly erected on a level piece of grassy ground and the Indian agent, Captain Frank Edwards, wasted no time in getting down to business. A long line formed in front of the main tent. Bea and I spent a solitary afternoon and evening on our island. Not a soul came near us. Next morning, the payment continued, but by afternoon, quite a few of the Indians came over to trade and I had to be quick on my feet.

On the third morning, Bea and I paddled over to the reserve to see what was going on. Captain Edwards and his clerk sat behind a flag-draped table. As each head of family stepped forward, he presented his treaty card. The clerk checked it against his records and when the size of the family was verified, the money was handed over in crisp, new one-dollar bills. Two Royal Canadian Mounted Police constables were in attendance, standing guard over the treaty money, which was carried around in leather satchels.

In another tent, the Indian Affairs' doctor was busy with a steady stream of patients. Tooth pulling seemed to be his main occupation. The sufferer sat down in a chair and pointed to the offending tooth or teeth. No anaesthetic was used. The doctor gave a quick yank with the forceps and called, 'Next please.' The doctor also issued a large amount of ordinary medicines on request, mostly aspirin or emetics.

During a lull in the proceedings, the doctor explained to us that his two great worries with regard to the Indian people were tuberculosis and scrofula or 'King's Evil'. Tuberculosis was prevalent among the Indians. They congregated in small, overheated shacks during the winter and the disease could spread quickly. Those afflicted refused to be taken out to sanitariums for treatment. They believed that if they went out to a hospital, they would die. And they wanted to stay at home and die peacefully among their families. So the disease spread. In later years, the Department of Indian Affairs waged a long, hard battle against it. Teams of experts went to every reserve in Canada and X-rayed everyone.

The other disease, scrofula, seemed to be peculiar to the Grassy Narrows Band. I hadn't noticed it among any other Indians. It took the form of large, angry scars and sores on either side of the throat. 'As long as the scars stay on the outside,' the doctor explained, 'the patients are all right. But once the disease moves inside, then it is only a matter of time.' He expressed the opinion that it came about as a result of generations of intermarriage.

Canon Sanderson accompanied the treaty party and he and Father Lemire were busy mingling with their flocks.

Around eleven o'clock, payment had been completed. Next on the agenda was the annual council meeting. The chief and the councillors were either re-appointed or replaced, and matters of general interest to the band, including any complaints, were brought to the attention of the Indian agent. This meeting was no concern of ours, so Bea and I returned to our island.

The council meeting must have gone on for a long time, as it was very late in the evening before Captain Edwards and his party came over to visit us. He apologized for the shortness of his visit, but explained that he was on a tight schedule and had many reserves to visit during the short two-month period. The tents were taken down next morning and the treaty party left.

Until the supply of treaty money dried up, I was kept on the hop in the store waiting on customers. I heaved a sigh of relief when I packed up all the cash I had in my safe, made out a remittance and sent it by mail to District Office. I wasn't comfortable with such a large amount of money on hand, even if the bulk of it was in crisp, new one dollar bills.

Gradually, the white tents on the reserve started to disappear as families slipped out in their canoes for the summer. First, the non-residents departed; then all the young men and their families. Most of them worked as guides at the fishing lodges or they got odd jobs, such as working with the section gangs on the railroad. Many of the families picked blueberries which grew in profusion everywhere. They were purchased by itinerant buyers and shipped to market in Winnipeg.

Finally, the reserve was deserted, except for a few of the older families who stayed all summer. They lived off the country, subsisting mainly on fish caught in their nets which they tended daily.

The older women made moccasins and often came over to the store with a few pairs at a time. I bought them as trade goods, intending to sell them the following winter to the trappers.

*   *   *

The summer of 1936 was a scorcher. According to the radio, people were trying to fry eggs on the sidewalk in front of the Free Press Building in Winnipeg. Bea and I thoroughly enjoyed the heatwave and almost lived in our swimsuits. We spent hours in our canoe, paddling around exploring the shores of the lake and the river in the vicinity of the post. These trips were made in the early morning or late evening hours when the winds were cooler.

Many mornings we watched muskrats swimming about quietly among the reeds in a shallow bay, or a mother mallard marshalling her brood of young along the shore in search of food. We saw the occasional deer come down to the water's edge to drink and then, startled by our silent approach, scamper back into the safety of the wood.

In the evenings, we drifted along quietly and listened to the weird cry of the loon. Once heard, this cry is never forgotten. A long, melancholy wail, bursting suddenly into a shriek of maniacal laughter. Even today, when I hear it, I get shivers up my spine, for it brings back almost forgotten memories. The cry of the loon, to me, is the call of Canada.

Occasionally, an Indian family returned from the track to spend a couple of days hoeing their potato patch, and then slipped

Hugh and Beatrice Ross on the front porch of the fire rangers' cabin at Delaney Lake, 1936.

silently out again. Several canoe parties passed through, mostly Americans on fishing expeditions. They spent a couple of hours on our island purchasing supplies and visiting. One such canoeing party was a bunch of young men from the Great West Life Assurance Company in Winnipeg. Bea was delighted to find that several of them were old acquaintances from the Winnipeg Canoe Club. They camped overnight with us and I'm sure John Loon must have wondered why the lights in our windows shone until the early morning hours.

The three fire rangers were back at their station on the portage into Delaney Lake. They visited us about once a week in the evenings. Fortunately, we could hear the put-put of their outboard motor long before they came into view, and had sufficient time to change from our swimsuits to more conventional attire.

After many invitations, we decided to paddle down to visit them at their camp one Sunday. We left about ten o'clock in the morning. The weather was still hot and sultry and the surface of the lake was smooth as glass. The camp was only a few miles away, so we took our time exploring as we went. After an enjoyable afternoon and a very good dinner, we set out on the return trip. Before we were half way up the southern arm of the lake, the

weather changed. The wind came up and began to blow quite
strongly, accompanied by intermittent bursts of cold rain. We
were in no danger and by keeping to the lee shore of the arm,
continued to make good progress, until we came to the last point
before entering the main body of the lake itself. I decided it would
be prudent to have a look-see before rounding this point. We
beached the canoe, turned it over and, securing it firmly, went to
have a look.

The wind was blowing directly towards us and the lake was a
mass of whitecaps. Although we were both good swimmers, there
was no point in taking chances so we sat down to wait out the
weather. I got a good fire going and we huddled close to it, hoping
that the wind would drop so we wouldn't have to spend the night
out of doors, in the rain. Usually when there is a strong wind
blowing, it drops at sunset for half an hour or so; then it will either
blow again or die altogether. Sure enough, as the daylight slowly
waned, the wind started to drop. We jumped into our canoe,
paddled like mad around the point and made for home as quickly
as possible.

I had a visit from an indignant John Loon early next morning. He had seen us depart the previous morning but hadn't seen
us return. He was agitated and, using some English, some Indian
and lot of body language, described his relief on seeing the light
appear in the windows of our house after dark. 'It is not right,' he
said, 'that the boss should take chances of getting drowned.' He
implied that it was the responsibility of all the Indians, and him in
particular, to look after our safety. Moreover, if anything had
happened to us, the Indians would be sure to be blamed in some
way or other. I apologized sincerely for having caused him all the
worry and gave him my assurance that I wouldn't do such a
foolish thing again.

It was good to know that someone was keeping an eye on us.
Greatly mollified, John took his leave. He was a prime example of
a 'Hudson's Bay Indian'. He would never deal with a free trader
and always did his business with the Company. Although he
wasn't a very good hunter, he always paid his debt. One of John's
proudest possessions was a Hudson's Bay medal which he wore
pinned to his chest on all formal occasions. The medal had been

presented to him in 1920, when, as a member of a party of Indians representing the Grassy Narrows Band, he had attended the 250th anniversary celebrations of the Company in Manitoba, at Lower Fort Garry. He loved to describe how the Indian people, representing all the tribes in Canada, had paddled their canoes down the Red River to the Lower Fort.

With the continuing dry summer, there were many forest fires in the area. A pall of smoke hung over us for days and the smell of burning wood filled our nostrils. None hit close to us until about the middle of August, when I noticed an ominous plume of smoke to the southeast. The local fire ranger crew had already spotted the smoke and reported it to their head office. By late afternoon, we could see the forestry planes flying in and out with men and equipment. When the fire was located, our rangers showed us on the map just where it was: on the shores of a small lake from which a creek flowed northwest to join the English river, quite near the eastern end of the reserve. The rangers advised us that there was no need to worry; a crew of fire fighters from Minaki was already on the job and slowly they were getting it under control.

We heard an outboard approaching from the east and recognized the red canoe belonging to the Ontario Department of Forestry, but we were surprised and pleased when our old friend, Sid Turner, stepped ashore and greeted us. The fire was taking a little longer to bring under control than they had first figured and they were running short of some supplies. We packed work socks, gloves, tobacco, tea, bacon and other sundries into boxes. As they were loading, Sid turned to us and said, 'You know, all the gang from Minaki are over there fighting the fire. Why don't you come over this evening for a visit and stay the night. They'll all be glad to see you.' I looked at Bea and she nodded. Since the next day was Sunday and the store was closed, I said, 'Okay Sid, expect us for supper.'

'And we'll bring the dessert,' shouted Bea, as the canoe pulled away from the shore. She spent the next few hours baking saskatoon berry pies and in the afternoon, we loaded up our tent and blankets, positioned the pies carefully in the canoe and set out.

On the way, we made sure to stop at John Loon's house to

tell him where we were going and that we wouldn't be back until the following morning. 'That is good,' he said, 'Now I know where you will be. But be sure to come back early in the day in case it gets windy.'

We had spotted the mouth of the creek on a previous trip and had no difficulty in locating it again. Soon we reached the lake and the rangers' camp on the shore. We were just in time for supper and the pies were welcome. The boys helped me to set up the tent. They were glad to see us again and we sat around the campfire drinking tea and getting caught up on the local news at Minaki. They were all tired from fighting the fires and had an early night.

The camp was roused at dawn. After a quick breakfast, we paddled off. A gauzy mist slowly swirled around the reeds along the winding weed-grown creek; then as the sun rose, its light reflected off the dewdrops hanging precariously from the long stems. It was a magical time. Occasionally a duck rose from the reeds as we approached and flew away with loud squawks. We watched a massive bull moose delicately pick his way down to the water's edge to drink. Red-winged blackbirds whistled their cheerful song as they balanced with marvelous agility on the swinging bullrushes.

As we passed John Loon's house, we noticed him sitting outside and waved to him. He acknowledged our greeting with a dignified uplifting of his hand and then stalked back indoors. Obviously, he had been sitting there waiting for us to pass.

In season, our island provided us with all kinds of wild fruit. First to ripen were the delicious wild strawberries, which carpeted the ground. They made tasty preserves. Later on, bushes dripped with Saskatoon berries, delicious when eaten just as they were picked and even better when made into pies. There were pin cherries which, when made into jelly, were a great accompaniment to our winter roasts of venison or moosemeat. On a nearby island there were masses of blueberries so we packed a lunch and spent a day picking as many as we could carry. Peter loved these outings, rambling all over the island. As long as we were on an island, we didn't worry about him; he couldn't get lost. Every so often, Bea had a 'preserving' day and Peter and I were never too far from the house. Both of us were waiting for a 'piece' — freshly made preserves on a slice of home-made bread.

On our visit to the fire rangers' cabin on Delaney Lake, I had been impressed with the neatness of the grounds. All the paths were carefully lined with whitewashed stones and the walkways strewn with sand. Our wooden walkways, which connected our house with the store and the warehouses, were getting rather dilapidated and the stringers were rotting in places. I decided to emulate the fire rangers' layout and one day, I ripped up all the old sidewalk. It was a long job and in the middle of it, I was sorry I started. All the stones and the sand had to be wheeled up from the beach. But when I was finished, it certainly was a great improvement.

By the end of September, the Indians started drifting back from the track. The wild rice season was coming on and soon their potatoes would be ready for lifting. The wild rice crop was heavy that year. It was harvested by canoes, each manned by two people, as they worked their way through the rice beds. The person in the rear looked after the paddling. The one in the bow used two sticks to bend the long ears of rice over the gunwale and beat the grains off the stalk.

When a canoe load had been garnered, it was spread out in the sun to dry. Then, a little at a time, it was parched over a slow fire. Shallow pits, about a yard across, had been dug in the ground and lined with clay. Notched poles were driven in at each side of the hole and a stout crossbar firmly attached to the uprights. A quantity of the parched rice was placed in the hole and then an old woman wearing new moccasins climbed in. Grasping the crossbar firmly in her hands, she shuffled in a slow, deliberate, dancing movement until the husks were separated from the rice. The final step was to winnow the rice by tossing it in the air, so that the breeze would blow away the husks. Wild rice formed a large part of the Indian diet. I purchased any surplus quantities from them on a barter basis, to be sold back later during the winter months. It wasn't in demand as an epicurean delight in restaurants at that time; most of it was eaten by the Indians.

We got many wild ducks during the fall season, although I didn't do any shooting myself. The post was situated in the middle of reserve land and I didn't want to offend the Indians by doing any shooting on their property. Instead, we bought them as we needed them, already plucked and dressed.

Bea seemed to like wild game as well as I did. We could get all the venison and moosemeat we wanted, as well as duck and geese. There was only one thing at which she drew the line. One day, old Roderick Land brought us a young beaver carcass. She stuffed and roasted it but when she placed it in the centre of the dinner table, she pushed her plate away. 'I can't eat it. I can't even look at it,' she said. She got up from the table and walked to the window. Perplexed, I pressed her for a reason. 'It's going to sound stupid and you'll probably laugh, but when I put that beaver on its back in the roasting pan, it looked just like a baby.' She shuddered. 'You eat it. But if Roderick Land ever offers you another beaver, you can cook it yourself.' I enjoyed my meal immensely. Bea took a peanut butter and jelly sandwich and went for a walk with Peter until I was finished.

One day late in the fall, Davy Glenn, our pilot, asked me casually how the hunting was around Grassy Narrows. 'Pretty good,' I replied. 'Lots of deer around.'

'Enough game for American hunters to come up and shoot? We're getting a lot of inquiries about deer hunting and we would like to fly hunters in,' he explained. I told him that I was sure that any hunter could get his deer within a week and if he was lucky, maybe a moose or bear.

'The problem would be to outfit the hunters properly, Davy. I haven't any equipment for that — just the regular groceries.' I mulled it over for a while. 'What I could do is arrange for an Indian guide, using his canoe, tent and cooking equipment. Of course, the hunter would have to pay the guide himself. And I think I better set the tariff.'

'That sounds great! I'll make sure that they buy their hunting licences before I fly them in. These hunters are really keen to get away from the beaten path and to hunt in virgin territory.'

This was the beginning of a profitable business. The Indians were glad to go out as guides and the money they earned helped to keep them going until the trapping season started. We had quite a few hunters that season and they all got their deer. Some even shot a bear or moose. In actual fact, most of them could have had their deer on the first day away from the post, but I cautioned the Indians not to be too quick. 'Take them up and down the river for a couple of days before you actually start looking for game.'

During the hunting season, we had a visit from Bea's brother-in-law, Pat Ellwein. He had written in advance to make the arrangements and drove up from South Dakota to Winnipeg with his wife Louise. From Winnipeg, they drove on to Kenora and then flew into Grassy Narrows. And they had a surprise for us — Bea's mother and dad. It was the first time either of them had flown and once they were over their initial apprehension, they enjoyed the trip.

I sent Pat out with Michell Keesik on his hunt and we had a grand visit with the old folks. Mrs Dingle loved the post and confided to Bea, 'This is the kind of life I would have liked when I was a young girl.' She admired our house and exclaimed over the dazzling whiteness of the lime wash. When she realized that we had an inside toilet, she confessed that an outhouse was one aspect of living in the bush that didn't appeal to her. And wasn't it nice that we had some of the amenities? As we prepared the tea, Bea remarked wryly, 'Thank God we made all the repairs. If they had come for a visit last year, they'd have taken the plane right back to Winnipeg. And me with it.'

Even Father Dingle had to agree that his daughter was not really living like a savage. Whether he was feeling magnanimous because his hunting had been successful or he really meant it, we didn't know. I persuaded Bea to accompany them back to Winnipeg for a short visit. It would be a break for her before the winter set in. She spent the day before they left baking bread and pies so that I wouldn't starve while she was away.

The morning of their departure was cold and bitter with snow squalls. I watched the plane taxi south through the flurries in preparation to turning around and taking off into the strong north wind. I could hear the sound of the motor revving up in the distance. I couldn't see through the snow and there was no sign of the plane. Suddenly, it appeared out of the storm, taxiing slowly against the wind and pulling up again onto the beach.

When it was being turned around, a strong gust of wind had

caught the plane and thrown it against a submerged rock, denting one of the pontoons. Rather than take any risks, Davy Glenn decided to come back to the island to check the damage. It proved to be a small hole and after pumping out the pontoon, he was able to patch it.

By this time, the weather had worsened, so they all came up to the house for lunch and waited to see if there would be an improvement in conditions. When there was no let-up, they reluctantly agreed to put off their departure until the following day. I glumly watched my pies and buns disappearing during lunch and then dinner. The weather broke bright and clear next morning and they got away without difficulty.

While Bea was away, I busied myself marking all my annual stock which had been brought in from the railway. This was not the big job it had been back in 1930. Now I only ordered heavy groceries and hardware to come in by train. The whole operation took less than a week. All dry goods were now being flown in from Kenora. Although the cost per 100 pounds was a little higher, it paid in the end. I was able to keep the dry goods stocks rotating and present new merchandise to my customers. This meant that I ordered dry goods approximately once a month, cutting down on stocks on hand, thereby reducing the interest on capital charges considerably.

Bea returned shortly before freeze-up. She had had a good holiday, renewing acquaintances with her old friends and buying the things a woman considers necessary. 'You know honey, I never realized how noisy and smelly cities are', she said. She put her arms around my neck. 'But most of all, I'm glad to get back to my own home again. And you!'

Winter set in quickly and by mid-December, the lake was well frozen over and the planes were able to land on skis. I was now back in the usual post routine. The trappers had all been outfitted and sent off and by Christmas, the fur started to come in.

One day in late January, I was surprised to see young Dennis Foubister in the store. I had outfitted him, his father and his two brothers after New Year's and didn't expect to see them until the end of February at the earliest. After exchanging the usual greetings, I asked, 'Why are you back so early? I didn't expect you for another month at least. Did you run short of anything?'

'No,' he answered, 'but my father cut his foot with an axe and we brought him back.'

'Is it a bad cut?' I remembered only too well my bad experience with an axe.

'Yes. My father cannot walk. We brought him all the way back on the toboggan.' He seemed worried so I asked if he would like me to go over and take a look at it. 'Oh yes,' he replied. 'I'm sure my father would like that.'

I dashed into the house, told Bea where I was going and grabbed some bandages and supplies from the medicine chest. When I cut myself at One Man Lake, there had been no medical supplies available other than those I brought with me. The Company practice was to keep a complete medicine cabinet at every post but not at outposts. So this time I wouldn't need to use whisky as an antiseptic.

Dennis and I jumped on his toboggan and were soon over at his father's house, which was only a half mile from the post. Old Alex was lying in bed. As I looked at his injured foot swathed in dirty white cloths, I thought, 'This is going to be a tough one.' Visions of blood poisoning or gangrene flashed across my mind. I asked Mrs Foubister to heat up some water and started to remove the filthy wrappings. There was no swelling and the rest of the foot didn't seem inflamed. At least blood poisoning hadn't started. When the last of the bandages were removed, I found a mess of dirty, brown goo smeared over the wound. Gingerly, I wiped it away. Old Alex had a long, jagged cut in the fleshy part of his instep. I asked him to wiggle his toes. He did and I decided he hadn't broken any bones.

'What on earth is that brown stuff on your foot?' I asked.

'Anishinabi mushkiki,' he replied. 'Indian medicine. Very good stuff.'

'Yes, I'm sure it is good medicine, Alex, but what is it?' He explained that the Indians used the brown powder contained in puff balls which grew as a vegetable fungus in the bush. They applied it to any open cut. It stopped the bleeding and helped the wound to heal. I tried not to look too sceptical. I washed the foot, applied an antiseptic, a dressing and then neatly bandaged it.

'You'll be fine now, Alex,' I said. 'It should take a couple of weeks before you will be able to put your weight on it. I'll come over every second day and change the dressing.' This I did and he recovered nicely.

On one of my trips, as I sat talking to the old Indian after dressing the cut, I lit my pipe. 'You like to smoke the pipe?' he asked.

'Yes, I do. I find it very relaxing.'

'Well, I have an old pipe upstairs in my trunk which I would like to show you.' He called his wife and had her fetch it. It was an old red pipe-stone calumet, with three bands of metal beaten into the stem and bowl. The metal looked like pewter, probably from an old teaspoon or plate. There was a long, wooden stem which fitted into the pipe-stone.

'Where on earth did you get this?' I asked, as I turned it over in my hands.

'Oh, my father picked it up a long time ago near Sioux Lookout. It is an old Sioux pipe.' When I expressed surprise at this, he told me that, in the old days, the Sioux used to make raids from the Dakotas and Minnesota up into Ontario. The Ojibway watched for the coming of these war parties from a high bluff which overlooks the town of Sioux Lookout; the present-day name for this town is a literal translation of the Indian name for the rock.

'Here,' said old Alex, as he handed me the pipe. 'You take it. I want you to have it. You have been very good to me. You fixed my foot.' I demurred, but when he continued to press it on me, courtesy demanded that I accept his gift. Next time I visited him I brought over a handsome briar pipe and a supply of tobacco as a gift in exchange.

Many years later, I learned that the puff balls that Old Alex had used on his foot were probably more responsible for curing the wound than my ministrations had been. The brown powder in the puff balls contained a high percentage of penicillin.

January and February continued bitterly cold. According to the thermometer on the wall outside our back door, the temperature dropped as low as −54° Fahrenheit and seldom, if ever, did it rise above −40°. During this cold weather, the animals didn't move about and, as a result, the winter hunt was poor. When the trappers returned at the end of February, they were hard put to pay off their debts in full. To help them out, I set some of them to work cutting firewood. Many had begun to run short of food and other necessities. After cutting the logs, they dragged them to the shore and I had them haul the whole supply right into the post by dog-team. Doing it this way was a little more expensive, but it was the only thing I could think of to let the trappers earn some extra money. I couldn't have them running up more debt which they couldn't afford to pay. And I couldn't have them doing without food either. I also had them build an ice-house on the north side and fill it up with ice. During the past hot summer, there were times when Bea and I would have given almost anything for a really cold drink of water.

With the coming of spring and break-up, things changed for the better. The muskrat and beaver hunt was excellent and once again, all debts were paid up and the Indians were happy and well fed.

Throughout the winter, we had been busy making arrangements for our long delayed honeymoon. We had saved our pennies carefully. Fortunately, we were both thrifty and outside of the occasional bottle of whisky and tobacco for my pipe, we weren't too distracted from our plans, so that over two winters we had saved enough to have a really enjoyable holiday.

At the end of May, an apprentice clerk arrived to assume temporary charge of the post until a permanent manager could be appointed. We took a change of management inventory; I closed off the annual books and we packed the fur on hand for shipment to England.

We packed up all our personal belongings to be held in storage at Grassy Narrows until we found out where our next posting would be.

On one fine June day, we said farewell to all our Indian friends, who had come over to the island to see us off. Then, together with our dog, Peter, we flew out to Kenora en route to Winnipeg.

10

SCOTLAND: 1937

We spent the first few days in Winnipeg on a hectic shopping spree. During the past two years, we had worn out all our old clothes, so there were many kinds of things to be purchased. I can recall buying a fine, new suit for $12.50 and a brand new pair of leather shoes for $5.00. We had our pictures taken, filled out the passport applications and, after explaining to the authorities how short our time was, they agreed to have our passports forwarded to our ship in Montreal, directly from Ottawa. We left Peter with Bea's parents and on 17 June 1937, we took the train for the first part of our trip to Scotland.

In Montreal, we boarded the *Duchess of Bedford* — the same ship on which I had sailed to Canada — and a week later, we landed at Greenock on the Firth of Clyde. We caught a north-bound bus in Glasgow and travelling via Aviemore, arrived home in Rothes late the same evening.

My parents gave us a real Scottish welcome. They liked their new daughter-in-law and took to her right away. It was grand to be back home again. My sister Dorothy was very much the young lady and admired all Bea's new clothes. Even the oh-so-changeable Scottish weather behaved itself. I took Bea all over the village, meeting and talking to my old friends and drinking innumerable cups of tea. As she was strictly a coffee drinker, I thought this was the supreme sacrifice. She said afterwards that she must have drunk gallons of the stuff.

I'm afraid the locals looked askance at her at first. She was a foreigner in their midst. One old shopkeeper took me aside and said, 'Your wife. She's no' a Yankee, is she?' When I assured him that she was a Canadian, he was much relieved.

Our first appearance on the tennis courts caused lots of uplifted eyebrows. Bea's short, white tennis shorts were in great contrast to the demure, pleated, knee-length skirts that the local girls were sporting. When they found out that she could play tennis as well or better than most of them, they accepted her. We went all over the countryside seeing the sights: visited the county town of Elgin and my old school, went on a picnic at the seaside at Lossiemouth, and spent one weekend with my old schoolmaster, Mr A. B. Simpson, who was now the rector of Forres Academy.

By the end of three weeks, I was feeling a little upset. In the seven years that I had been in Canada, my old school friends and I had naturally drifted apart. They were quite willing to talk about the price of fish, the Aberdeen Football Club, the weather, even the abdication of Edward, Prince of Wales. But as far as Canada was concerned, they didn't know anything about it, nor did they want to hear about it from me. They were not interested in what I had been doing over there. They seemed to think, moreover, that because I had been abroad, I was now a millionaire and should be quite prepared to buy the rounds of drinks. When we went down to the pub that evening, and it happened again, I had enough.

'Bea, let's get out of here. Out of Rothes. Let's go and see the rest of Scotland and then go down to England.'

Bea was surprised at my suggestion, and even more at my reasons for it. She had been having a good time and just assumed that I was too. 'Do you think that it's fair to your parents to leave just like that? Your mum will be so disappointed. Why don't we stay another two weeks,' she pleaded. So I spent the time at home, watching a closeness develop between my mother and my wife, which gladdened my heart.

We left on a bus tour to Inverness and down the Great Glen past Loch Ness, where Bea spent an unsuccessful hour looking for the monster; then, to Fort William and Ben Nevis. She was so quiet as we drove over the hills to Aberdeen that I anxiously asked her if she were all right. 'I'm fine, darling. It's all just so incredibly beautiful.'

From Aberdeen, we went on to Edinburgh, visiting the palace at Holyrood and Edinburgh castle. Neither of us had ever been there and we could easily understand why it is considered one of the loveliest cities in the world. From there we caught a bus to London and spent the rest of our holidays seeing the sights of that great city.

We took the train to Liverpool for our return trip to Canada on the *Duchess of Bedford.* By this time, we had spent all our money and I had to wire District Office in Winnipeg to have $50.00 awaiting our arrival in Montreal.

Back in Winnipeg, I went down to Head Office, full of anticipation, to find out what my new posting would be. My district manager was again out of town so I asked Alec Anderson, the district accountant, where I was going.

'You're going back to Grassy Narrows,' he told me. I couldn't believe it. There had to be some mistake. 'But that's impossible,' I exclaimed. 'Mr Parsons promised me that I would get a new post and I have no intention of going back to Grassy Narrows.'

'Sorry, but that's the way it is. The positions for the year have all been approved and you're slated for Grassy Narrows.'

'Not on your life,' I replied. 'I want to see the Commissioner.'

'I'm afraid you can't do that, but maybe you could talk to the fur trade controller,' he suggested. The fur trade controller told me the same story. I was going back to Grassy Narrows and no, he couldn't arrange for me to see the fur trade commissioner. But he too had a suggestion. 'Why not go and see the new man who has been appointed personnel manager.' By this time, I was livid and I stormed out of the building and went back to break the bad news to Bea.

'I'm not going back to Grassy Narrows,' I yelled. 'I'll quit the Company first.'

After she had calmed me down a bit, Bea said, 'Marian Ross was in the office when Mr Parsons promised you a move, wasn't she?' When I agreed, she continued. 'All right then, let's not be too hasty. We'll wait until this evening and I'll telephone Marian when she gets home from work. Maybe she'll be able to do something about it.'

For the rest of the day, I paced the floor, worrying about our future, but certain in my own mind that I wasn't going back to Grassy Narrows. Bea tried to take my mind off the problem, and I did make the effort, but she could see that I was very upset.

Marian listened quietly when I spoke to her that evening. 'Don't worry,' she said. 'You come to the office and be in the hallway outside Mr Parson's office at ten o'clock sharp, and I'll see if I can get you in to see him.' At the appointed time I was sitting on a chair in the hallway of Hudson's Bay House. Marian winked as she walked past me into the office. In a couple of minutes, she came out again to say that her boss would see me. Later, she told us that all she said to him was, 'Mr Ross from Grassy Narrows is back from his holidays in Scotland. He's outside in the hall now, waiting to discuss his next posting.'

When I walked in, Mr Parsons greeted me. 'Well, Ross, did you enjoy your holidays?'

'Very much sir. But you were right. Three months was long enough. I was glad to get back to Canada.'

'And where are you being posted to now?'

'Back to Grassy Narrows,' I answered very quietly. Then, unable to control myself, I blurted out, 'I won't go back there again.' Surprised by my outburst, he first looked annoyed and then, realizing my destination, he jumped out of his chair.

'That's absurd. If I recall rightly, I promised you a new posting, didn't I?' I nodded. 'Right. You come back here in half an hour while I find out what's going on.' I left his office, left the building and walked round and round the outside of Hudson's Bay House until I figured the time was up.

'Ross, I am appointing you to the charge of Temagami Post. It is a big post and an important one. It will be up to you to make a go of it,' he warned.

Temagami! I could scarcely believe my ears. Temagami was the biggest post in the district. Besides being a fur post, it was the centre of a large summer resort area, catering to American visitors. In fact, it was the plum of the district. Overjoyed, I pumped his hand and babbled my thanks. 'It won't be my fault if I don't make a go of Temagami,' I promised.

'Ross,' he said, looking straight through me with his steely eyes, 'if you don't make a go of Temagami, it most definitely will be your fault. Remember that.'

All I could do was agree with a meek, 'Yes, sir.'

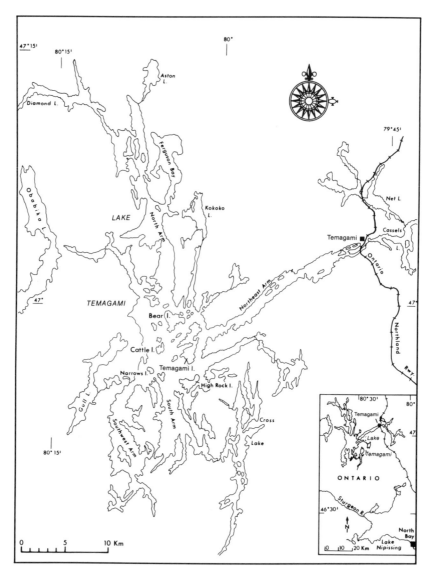

Map of Lake Temagami. This spelling was traditional in Company records, although the spelling 'Timagami' is used on some modern maps.

11

TEMAGAMI: 1937-1941

Lake Temagami is a large body of water about 100 miles north of North Bay, Ontario. Four long arms stretch out from the centre like the spokes of a wheel. In the middle are four islands: Temagami, Cattle, Garden and Bear. The settlement where the local people lived and where the Hudson's Bay post was built was on Bear Island.

In days gone by, there was no permanent post there, but a wintering outpost known as Flying Post, operated either from Abitibi or Temiskaming. Seasonally run, the location would be changed as the Indians moved around their trapping grounds. With the building of the Temiskaming and Northern Ontario Railway from North Bay to Moosonee, Lake Temagami had been developed as a summer tourist resort. Indians had gradually come there to find jobs as guides and in time, the settlement of Bear Island came into being and the Company post was permanently stabilized. There was no Indian reserve and most of the local people were half-breeds who originally came from the James Bay area around Moose Factory.

The village of Temagami stood at the easterly end of the north-east arm of the lake where the railway passed by on its way north. We got off the train at the station and caught the steamer *The Belle of Temagami,* which made a daily trip during the summer up the lake with mail, provisions and passengers. In a few hours' time, we rounded Turner's Point and there was the post. The steamer tied up at the Company's dock and as I gazed at the varied large buildings, I must confess that I had a few misgivings. Was I going to be able to handle a post of this size? It was quite a responsibility for a young man.

The dock was a huge plank affair jutting out into the lake; it was at least 25 feet wide and sat four feet above the water on three large log cribs, filled with rock. In the middle of it was a gas pump for motorboats. The gas container tanks were underneath the dock. To the left was a large, two-storey boathouse with a small, sloping dock in front for canoes. To the right was an L-shaped dock built by the provincial government, and beyond that, a two-storey frame building.

A huge warehouse stood to the left of the store and behind it, were sundry outbuildings. What a difference it was from Grassy Narrows! Bea squeezed my hand as we walked off the boat.

The purser introduced me to Peter Norby, the boat-house man who was busy unloading freight. 'You go on up to the store,' he said. 'I'll look after your luggage and take it up to the house.' He indicated a large white frame building. We walked up the gangway to the store which was full of people. The clerk behind the counter pointed out George Linklater and I went over and introduced myself. George had been the assistant at the post for a number of years. Mr S. R. Thorpe, the previous post manager, had died in a tragic drowning accident six weeks before our arrival. George had been acting as temporary manager until a new man was appointed. After he unsmilingly turned over the keys to the house, I told him that Bea and I would go over there, get settled in, and that I would see him the next morning at nine o'clock when the store opened.

There had been another store at Temagami, built along the same lines as the Minaki store, with an apartment above for the manager. It had burned to the ground in the fall of 1936 and a new store had been built during the winter months to be ready for business in the spring. Unfortunately, a manager's suite had not been built upstairs; instead there were three bedrooms and a modern bathroom for the use of summer staff. About this time, the Company was engaged in an extensive rebuilding program throughout all posts in the North, but Head Office, in their wisdom, had decided that the former staff house at Temagami would do for the manager's quarters. They did have plans to build a new house; time proved that this project was not high on their priority list, for each year the new dwelling was deferred. We were

Regatta Day at Lake Temagami, undated. This store burned down in 1936, the year before the Ross's arrival.

still living in the staff house when I received my next posting in the fall of 1941.

The house was well built and in a good state of repair. What is more, it proved to be warm and comfortable during the winter months. We entered through a summer kitchen that was equipped with a cookstove, table and chairs, and a sink with a hand pump. No more hauling water from the lake, I thought. Wrong! The pump could only be used during the season of open water. As soon as there was a sign of the lake freezing over, it was dismantled and I was back to carrying water again.

The main floor was made up of a kitchen, small dining-room and a large living-room with a window overlooking the lake. Bea and I were delighted with the view and the layout. A door from the living-room opened out to a screened veranda. Upstairs there were three large bedrooms. All the interior walls were the usual tongue-in-groove lumber, stained a dismal brown. Bea walked around the house, upstairs and down, mentally re-arranging the furniture and deciding just where our things should be placed. She would make a suggestion; I'd agree and before I could turn around, she had changed her mind. Finally, she agreed to stop fretting, took off her hat and we stood for a long time just admiring the view from our front window.

For the next month or so, my spare time was fully occupied helping Bea who was working like a Trojan on the house. We painted all the ceilings white and applied several coats of pastel-coloured Alabastine to the walls. The current year's budget included a reasonable figure for furniture replacement. Bea wrote away for catalogues and we spent many hours poring over them. Finally we ordered a dining-room suite, a chesterfield and two armchairs, all in colonial maple. I also ordered a new heater which burned coal briquettes. No more lugging cordwood for me!

By the time the new furniture arrived, the things that had been placed in storage at Grassy Narrows were delivered. Bea hung new curtains and soon, with all our bits and pieces around us, we had a cheery comfortable home.

As the busy summer season was over, George Linklater and I went ahead with the change of management inventory, while the apprentice clerk handled the day-to-day trading in the store. It went smoothly. As we went along, all seasonal merchandise — fishing tackle, summer clothing, souvenirs — was packed in cartons and stored upstairs in the warehouse. Because of the fire which had destroyed the store the previous year, all the merchandise was current and saleable, with one exception. We had in stock twenty-four ladies' Hudson's Bay blanket coats without collars, a style which hadn't gone over with the tourists at all. I wrote them off completely.

With the inventory completed, customers' accounts all checked and verified, and the cash balanced, I formally took over the management of Temagami Post. It was now the end of September, and the apprentice clerk left; George and I were alone to run the store. It was brand new and efficiently planned — a manager's dream.

Built at the top of the slope overlooking the lake, it was approached by a short flight of steps to a large veranda. The front entrance was flanked by two large, plate-glass, display windows. Inside, in the trading area, the shelves were all adjustable. Instead of long counters, there were display tables on the dry goods side

The manager's house at Lake Temagami, 1937.

and modern groceteria gondolas on the other side. At the rear, the manager's office — fully equipped with an adding machine and typewriter — was on one side, and the post office on the other. I was postmaster too.

Beneath the whole length of the store was a roomy, full-sized basement. Most of one side was used for storing canned goods which were piled on raised wooden platforms. At the end of the room was a smaller cold storage room where barrels of apples, sacks of potatoes, onions and turnips could be kept free of frost. An engine room and a furnace room took up the other side. The furnace room held a large, wood-burning, hot-air furnace which heated the whole building. It had sufficient space to store the winter's supply of cordwood.

The engine room held an Onan 32-volt electric power plant which provided our electricity. Two banks of 2-volt glass battery cells lined one wall — eight cells to a bank. The plant was entirely automatic, cutting in by itself when the batteries were low and stopping once they were recharged. All that had to be done was to make sure that the gas tank was kept filled. Once a month, it was necessary to give these batteries a complete recharge. The plant was switched from automatic to manual, the tops of each cell were removed and the engine run until the cells were bubbling freely. Then the plant continued to run for a further two-hour period until the complete recharging had been accomplished.

In another corner was a water pump, connected to a well which was bored into the ground from the basement. This, together with the automatic water pressure tank, supplied the water for the upstairs bathroom.

Most of the first floor of the large, oblong, two-storied warehouse was taken up with the storage of non-freezeables, with a separate area for flour and cereals. At the rear were two smaller rooms: one, a general workshop where our tools were kept and the other, a locker room for use by canoe parties to store their city clothes before embarking on canoe trips.

The second storey of the warehouse was one huge room with deep shelving for our reserve stocks of dry goods and hardware on one side. A number of tables and garment racks at the back held our reserve supplies of Hudson's Bay blankets, windbreakers and Red River coats. The other side of the room held the rental equipment, used in the outfitting of canoeists. There were all kinds of cooking utensils, tumplines, axes, grub boxes, tents and blankets.

Down by the dock, the boat-house held our rental canoes and wooden skiffs. There were approximately sixty-five canoes, all canvas covered, made by the Chestnut Canoe Company of Fredericton, New Brunswick; and about twelve wooden square-sterned skiffs with an equal number of outboard motors.

The boat-house was the sole domain of our boatman, Peter Norby. He was a thick-set, barrel-chested Norwegian with piercing blue eyes and a mop of fair curly hair. He wore an imposing moustache which branched out from either side of his face — the epitome of an ancient Viking. After serving his apprenticeship as a carpenter in Norway, Peter had gone to sea, sailing all the oceans of the world, including the Arctic and Antarctic oceans aboard whaling vessels. He learned to speak English on board British ships and some of the fo'c's'le expressions that he used in the course of everyday conversation were enough to curl your hair. After one conversation with Peter, Bea quietly asked me 'Did Peter really say what I thought I heard?' I had to laugh. She

Boatman Peter Norby. 1937.

hadn't batted an eye at the time. Despite his salty language, he was a well-educated and well-read gentleman and we both became very fond of him. He lived in a small cabin behind the post buildings and only worked for us during the summer season. In the winter, he moved to an island several miles away. He owned the island and was saving up enough money to go into the mink-ranching business. To this end, he was busy building a house and the quarters required for breeding mink.

*   *   *

Bear Island was quite large, sloping gently upwards from the east and south sides. On the west was a large flat area used as a baseball diamond. The ground rose up sharply to the north, ending in a high, rocky hill on top of which was perched a fire lookout tower. The main settlement ran from the Hudson's Bay property along the shore to John Turner's hotel. Beyond were a few houses, ending with the buildings of the Ontario Forestry Branch. Farther back were the Anglican Church, the schoolhouse and the Roman Catholic Church. The Anglican Church was only open in the summer season when a divinity student was sent up from Toronto. Father Wittig, the young Roman Catholic priest, was stationed on the island all year around, as he was also the schoolmaster.

Little by little we got to know the people. It didn't take us long to find out that Granny Turner was the matriarch of the district. Little went on without her knowing about it or giving her consent to it. When we paid her a visit, we found her to be a delightful old lady: short and plump, with gray hair which she parted in the middle and pulled tightly back into a bun. She and her late husband had started the hotel — a first-class tourist business. It was run by her son, John, known locally as Small-boy. Her brother-in-law, George Turner Sr., and his wife Angele lived close by. Granny Turner had two other sons on the island: Larry, who worked as a guide and boatman; and George, Jr., who worked for a commercial camp.

Not far from us lived Joe Lanoie and his wife, Olive. Joe was one of those irrepressible French Canadians — always bubbling over with good humour. He was a hard worker and looked after several private cottages; he guided for the owners in the summer and put up their ice and wood in the winter. Olive was typically English, and we spent many Sunday afternoons having a 'proper English tea' at their house. Both of them were deeply superstitious and studied their horoscopes seriously. No matter how good the weather was in the winter, if Joe's horoscope warned that it was going to be a bad day for him, he stayed in bed. During the summer, Olive ran a small tearoom.

Another of our neighbours was Mrs Elsie Groves who ran a small store during the summer. She carried soft drinks, candies and tobacco mainly, and only a few groceries. In time, we became friends with Elsie and her husband who was a teacher in Guelph, Ontario. There was no hint of business rivalry between us.

The only government employee on the island was Herb Price. He was employed by the Ontario Forestry Branch and in the summer, he took his turn working in the fire tower with the other seasonal forestry employees. During the winter, he was a telephone linesman and kept a constant check on the line owned and operated by the Forestry Branch, that ran between Bear Island and the village of Temagami. It was a typical bush line, strung on insulators between trees or on poles across from the island to the mainland and along behind the northeast arm of the lake. Herb spent many hours tramping along on snow-shoes in

Lakeview Hotel, managed by John 'Smallboy' Turner at Lake Temagami. Undated, but prior to summer 1937.

the winter, repairing breaks brought about by heavy ice conditions.

Other than the phone in the forestry building, which was closed during the winter, the only other telephone was in our store. It was connected to the forestry line in the village, to the local doctor, the post office and the train station. There was no connection to the outside world. Only in case of emergency would the forestry office hook up our telephone to the outside system. During the winter, I was called upon at all hours of the night and day to ring up the doctor. Quite often I could see that the calls were not urgent or even necessary. But Dr McGowan advised me never to refuse a call. He was one of many dedicated doctors I met in the bush. He assured me that he was always at home or in his office and would accept every call.

There were hundreds of islands scattered over the lake. Some were owned by people from Toronto or the southern Ontario area but a lot of them were owned by Americans. Besides the private cottages, there were many commercial fishing lodges and several holiday camps — some only for adults and a few for young people and youth groups. A few miles to the north on Garden Island, a crusty old Englishman named Harry Smith and his wife operated a camp and lived on the island the year around. Two Toronto couples — Fred and Phyllis Dinsmore and Red and Audrey Spittal — operated Temagami Lodge just south of us on Temagami Island. Dewey Desrosiers ran Camp Ogama on the south side of the island. Dewey, another effervescent French Canadian, spent many winters prospecting all over the northern country and insisted that someday he would strike it rich. He did, and not too many hundreds of yards from his own camp, becoming very rich indeed. That winter, the Dinsmores and the Spittals remained at the camp to start up a mink ranch. We became friends with the two couples and visited them often.

The *Belle of Temagami* ceased its daily runs in the middle of October. Instead of the daily mail service, we received mail only on Saturdays. In winter the Company had a contract to carry mail to and from the village. Since there were no dogs at the post, I had to hire a team to make the trip. It was a chancy business, as sometimes the dog-team owners would be away from home visiting their traplines. Often it was a problem trying to locate and hire a team to make the weekly mail trip. I resolved that the following winter, I would have a team of my own.

Although the local people talked Ojibway amongst themselves, they always spoke English when they came to the store. I found that, although it wasn't the same as the Ojibway I had learned at Grassy Narrows, their speech had a similar ring. Basically it was the same, but there were many different turns of phrase and intonations, with a smattering of words derived from the French. At Grassy Narrows, a quarter was *payjik shuniass* meaning 'one small piece of silver'. Here, a quarter was *payjik transo*. *Transo*, I figured, was from the French *trente sous*.

I listened carefully to all the conversations and in a short time, I could understand everything they said. But I never let on that I could speak Ojibway or understand it. We had several dear old ladies who congregated in the store regularly and chattered away among themselves in their own language. They used to criticize me up and down, discuss everything I did — good or bad, whether I would make a go of being manager at Temagami or if I was too young for the job. They even speculated on why Bea and I had no children and what I wore to bed. As I listened to them expound on my virtues or lack of them, there were times when I had to hurry from the store to keep myself from laughing out loud at some of their outrageous suppositions. Their criticisms weren't confined to me. Everyone in town was fair game.

The local people were still well heeled from their summer employment, so I put on a special sale in case lots of groceries. I loaded the display windows with sacks of flour and sugar, cases of milk, canned fruits and vegetables, and used large display tags showing the cut prices. George, my assistant, wasn't too happy with the idea. It had never been done before. But the customers liked it. I explained that all the sale prices were 'cash only'. If they couldn't store the cases they bought, we would store them in the warehouse with their names written on the goods. They could pick up the merchandise as needed. For the next week we did a roaring trade.

Mr Thorpe, my unfortunate predecessor, had been in charge of the post for many years and had been well liked and respected. Because of this, it soon became evident that I had a problem. People were accustomed to Mr Thorpe's way of doing business. I got tired of hearing 'Mr Thorpe didn't do it that way' from my customers and George. Unfortunately, no matter what I asked him to do, he always referred to 'Mr Thorpe's way.' It wore me down. Bea and I discussed it at length.

'I realize George is much older than you, Hugh, and you feel funny about it. But after all, you are the boss and he has to understand that.'

I decided to see if time would make things easier, but the situation only worsened, so I called George into the office and brought matters to a head.

'Things can't go on like this, George. I realize that my way of doing things varies from Mr Thorpe's but, in case you have forgotten, I am in charge of this post and from now on, I want things done my way.'

George Linklater was usually a taciturn man, but now it all came out. He was very unhappy. He didn't like working for a younger man and didn't see why I should come in and change the routines that had been working well for so many years. And then finally, he came to the crux of the matter. He said that after all his years at Temagami, he felt that he should have been put in charge of the post and not me.

'I'm sorry you feel this way, George,' I said, relieved that at last the air was cleared. Perhaps we could work things out now. 'As I see it, there are only two things you can do. Either make up your mind to work for me or I'm afraid you will have to resign.'

George chose to resign. In many ways he had been a great help to me, so I was sorry to lose his experience. I forwarded his resignation to District Office and explained that I could manage the store alone during the winter but would require an apprentice clerk in the spring.

*   *   *

We did a steady business in the store. I wasn't overworked but I had enough to do. The only really busy day was Saturday —mail day. Everyone in town came in to collect their mail. Occasionally the mailman would be held up by bad weather and was late in returning, which meant that the store stayed open late in the evening, until the mail had all been sorted and distributed. I didn't particularly like this, as it meant I had to be at the store past the start of 'Hockey Night in Canada.'

The following winter, with the consent of the local people, I arranged with the post office department that the weekly mail day be switched from Saturday to Friday. This meant that people coming in from outlying areas for their mail on Saturday would get it promptly and wouldn't have to wait around the store for hours.

On 24 December we held the Christmas shoot, an annual event at Temagami. Everyone in the district gathered at the store to watch the various competitions which ran from .22 calibre rifles at 25 yards, to large calibre rifle shoots at targets spaced from 100 to 400 yards out on the lake ice. The men were pretty fair shots and the competition was keen. Most of the prizes, I noticed, were being won by either Donald McKenzie or Tommy Potts. Both of them had served in the Canadian Army during World War I. Donald McKenzie, in fact, had been a sniper. My part in the proceedings was small. I supplied the targets and awarded grocery prizes for the competitions. The grand prize was a pair of Hudson's Bay blankets, awarded to the competitor who amassed the most points overall.

My coterie of dear old ladies was in their usual corner, gossiping away. I eased my way over to them and casually joined in their conversation, in their own language. Slowly the conversation died and a look of consternation came over their faces.

'Oh, my,' said one of them, giggling nervously with her hand covering her mouth. 'You have been listening to us all the time. You know what we have been saying about you.' I nodded in agreement and they all got very flustered, like a flock of hens disturbed by a fox.

'Now, now, ladies, don't worry your heads about that,' I said, soothingly. 'As a matter of fact, you have been a big help to me. Do you realize it would have taken me ten years to learn about the people here? I'm new to the post and many of the things you said were true and helpful and I appreciate knowing them.' This mollified them somewhat but to ease their embarrassment, I added, 'Ladies, I have a very special deal for you. Do you remember those Hudson's Bay coats I have in the warehouse?' I had their interest now. 'I'm sure you are all good sewers and could make them into sensible parkas or windbreakers. If you can do that, I'm prepared to let you have them at a very reasonable price.'

They got into a huddle in a corner and talked it over. Then one old lady looked at me shrewdly and said, 'Yes, we could do that.' She hesitated, but at the urging of her friends, she asked, 'What do you mean by a very reasonable price?'

'How much do you offer?' I countered.

Maggie Moore looked at me slyly. 'I wouldn't give you more than $5.00 for one.' Since I had written them off completely, I quickly answered, 'You're on.' Before they could change their minds, I went into the warehouse to get the coats. In no time, they were all snapped up. Maggie bought four coats — one for herself and one for each of her three daughters. As they made their way to the door, convinced that they had the best of the deal, I opened the front door for them and said in a quiet conspiritorial voice, 'Ladies, I just want you to know, since you were so curious, I only wear pyjamas to bed in the winter.' They giggled behind their hands and as they scurried from the store with their booty, I called after them, 'Mind you, I don't want that spread all over the village.'

Temagami was not a big fur-producing post. This was a great disappointment to me. I liked buying fur and wanted to keep my grading eye in practice. To be sure, there was fur to be purchased but nothing to compare with the volume I had bought at Grassy Narrows. I missed the fall outfitting of trappers and the wait until they came in at Christmas with their catch. Here, trapping was merely a sideline, to be indulged in when the weather was good or there was no other work to be found. The winter mainstay of the local men was cutting ice and cordwood for the many camps and cottages on the lake. Instead of getting trapping advances, they ran monthly accounts in the store.

George Turner, Sr. was one of the main contractors in these businesses and he employed most of the local men. He owned a horse, wood sleighs and a gasoline-powered saw. He had the contract for putting up the wood and ice for the post.

There was a great difference in the weather at Temagami. The winters were shorter and much milder than in northwestern Ontario. We were subjected to sudden and severe changes in temperature. Almost overnight, we would have a warm spell, lasting for days. Sometimes it even rained, and much of the snow would disappear from the bush. Practically all the snow would go from the ice on the lake. When there was glare ice, cars would travel on the lake up from the village of Temagami; but great care had to be taken, for during a warm spell, large cracks would develop on the lake, showing open water several yards wide. One of the local men explained that we were situated in a severe weather trough that stretched from James Bay to the Great Lakes.

On our regular weekly mail trips, we always used the bush trail that followed the telephone line and a chain of small lakes, rather than going across the lake. While it was uphill and down-hill on the portages, it was much shorter. Halfway to the village there was a lumber camp with a well-maintained ice road for the log-hauling. More important, the cooks there were obliging and we could always get a hot meal.

After New Year's, Bea accompanied Joe and Olive Lanoie on a trip out to Toronto. It made a welcome break for her and she was able to visit her relatives. It was a long three weeks. While she was away, I had time to reflect on just how special a woman had to be to marry and live in the bush, in always less than elegant accommodation, without seeing another white woman for months at a time, and coping with situations completely new to her and for which she had almost no preparation.

In the spring of 1938 we were fully occupied in preparing merchandise requisitions for the summer. At least 60 per cent of our annual sales were made during the three short summer months and it was essential that we have sufficient goods on hand. Merchandise had to be ordered for delivery right after open water; this gave us time to unpack and price it in time for the tourist rush. It was a long job and entailed much study of the previous season's invoices. Groceries and the usual dry goods and hardware were easy, but tourist merchandise was something else again.

Our main selling lines were Hudson's Bay blankets — red and multi-striped were the most popular — Hudson's Bay wind-breakers, parkas and Red River coats. Viyella shirts in authentic clan tartans were ordered from Gerhard-Kennedy in Winnipeg. Our cheaper line of plaid shirts and a special line of red flannel shirts called 'Robin' brand, were ordered from the Deacon Shirt Company in Belleville, Ontario. Ladies' sealskin slippers from Henry Ross in Loretteville, Quebec, sold well, and so did men's Shogomocs, a type of oiled, leather, factory-made moccasin. Our Fur Sales Department in Montreal provided us with an assort-ment of dressed furs — mainly white, red and silver foxes; and a few wolf and black bear skins which were quickly snapped up for rugs.

From our Montreal merchandise depot, we received an assortment of Eskimo carvings, both in soapstone and ivory. This was a long time before Eskimo art and handicrafts became well known and sought after in world markets. The carvings were bought at the Company's posts in the Arctic, from Eskimos who worked on them when the weather wasn't good for hunting.

Our biggest supplier of native handicrafts was a Mrs Alston who had a store in Little Current on Manitoulin Island in Lake Huron. We purchased a large quantity of birchbark baskets, beautifully decorated with dyed porcupine quills; sweetgrass baskets, and miniature birchbark canoes.

I bought all the beadwork moccasins and mitts that the local women could produce and augmented this stock with supplies from neighbouring posts. We didn't carry any of the shoddy imported souvenirs which are now sold in many tourist spots.

Finally, all the requisitions were completed with the exception of our fishing tackle assortment. Lake Temagami was noted for its fishing — mainly pickerel, smallmouth bass and lake trout. There was also excellent fishing for brook trout at the Lady Evelyn trout streams, about forty miles from the post. My knowledge of sport fishing was nil but I struggled along, trying to make up an order. Then a travelling salesman from Alcock, Laight and Westwood of Toronto, our main fishing-tackle supplier, telephoned me from the village. He was making his regular calls in the district and wanted to come up that afternoon.

We invited him to stay overnight and that evening he made up my complete order, guaranteeing that he would take back any items I could not sell and give me full credit for them. His knowledge of sport fishing helped me immeasurably and I owe him a deep debt of gratitude. Over the years, I learned the art of angling and ultimately was able to advise on many aspects of the sport.

I particularly enjoyed casting for smallmouth bass. In my opinion this was the best sport fishing of all. Lake Temagami is large with many deep spots where the big lake trout lurk at the bottom. But I did not have the patience to troll slowly up and down, hour after hour, with 200 feet of copper line dangling from a short stubby rod.

Then there were the night crawlers or dew worms. At home in Scotland, we used to mix up a quantity of dry mustard in a pail of water and pour it over a bit of lawn. I guess the worms didn't like the mustard, as they came to the surface fairly quickly and we

Apprentice clerk Arthur Howarth on his way to the water hole in the frozen lake. The manager's house is in the background. 1939.

grabbed them for fishing. But at Temagami, dew worms were big business. They were shipped to us daily from Toronto, packed live in small wooden boxes containing moss and cornmeal and covered with burlap.

With the spring came an ever-increasing volume of correspondence, mainly in connection with the outfitting of canoe trips. Grub and equipment lists were sent out to the many inquirers, together with information on the different varieties of fishing available and suggested itineraries. When each trip was finalized, canoes and guides had to be reserved against various starting dates. I handled the correspondence myself, with a 'hunt and peck' system on the typewriter that was slow but adequate for the job.

*   *   *

Shortly before break-up, District Office sent me an apprentice clerk, Art Howarth. He was a Winnipeg boy; this was his first posting and he was my first apprentice clerk. Bea and I liked the lad very much. He remained at Temagami for eighteen months and was, in every respect, a first-class employee.

Three university students arrived from Winnipeg in early June to work during the summer. They were Brian and Ian Robertson, sons of the fur trade controller, and another student named Dan. They were the first of a series of summer staff at Temagami. In later years, the staff included Glen Maconnell, a young lad from Head Office who eventually became a top fur buyer; Jack Anderson, son of District Manager J. W. Anderson; and David Parsons, son of the fur trade commissioner. Joe and Frank Wittig, younger brothers of the local priest; and Hugh Funnell, son of a Toronto professor who had a summer cottage on the lake, rounded out this group of young men. They worked their heads off for me.

District Office also sent up Matt Cook, who had come out with me from Scotland as an apprentice clerk in 1930. He had been injured going over a portage with his dogs and was still suffering from disc trouble. As he had spent a previous summer at Temagami, District Office thought his knowledge would be of great assistance to me, and they were right. He stayed until the end of September and I was sorry to see him leave.

The *Belle of Temagami* resumed its daily run up and down the lake and the tourist season was in full swing. The hours were long and the work hard, but we all pitched in and got it done. I worked out an hourly rotation for the staff. By working one double shift per week, each member was able to have a full weekend off each month. When they were at liberty, they were entitled to take a canoe or skiff and motor, free of charge, provided they let me know where they were going and when they expected to return.

Friday night was the busiest night of the week. Square dances were held at Turner's hotel and people came from all over the lake to attend. The docks were always lined with boats. The orchestra was strictly local — piano, violin and drums. Dress was almost a uniform: blue jeans, plaid shirt open at the neck, and a red bandana either tied around the neck or tied at the belt.

Interior of the Temagami store. Left, Glen Maconnell, Robert Turner or Boychee, Frank Wittig, Art Howarth and Hugh Ross.

On dance night, I closed the store at nine o'clock sharp, to enable the boys to attend. Each week, one of them stopped work at supper time and took my boat around the camps to collect the boys' dates. After the dance, the girls were delivered back the same way. As a result, there were no prolonged good-nights; otherwise the boat would not have been returned until the wee small hours.

By this time, I had acquired an inboard motor boat. I'm no mechanic and didn't like or have any faith in outboard motors. One Sunday afternoon in May, Bea and I had gone over to Temagami Lodge to have dinner with the Dinsmores. On our return trip, right in the middle of a stretch of open water, the outboard conked out. I couldn't restart the thing and had to row all the way home. The weather was fine and we weren't in any danger, but I decided then and there, I would get a proper boat to use in any kind of weather. I located one at Bracebridge, Ontario, and had it delivered to the dock at Temagami village for the inclusive price of $300.00. It was an old-fashioned lapstrake boat, twenty feet in length with a six-foot beam and a four-cylinder motor. It couldn't plane over the water at thirty miles an hour, crashing down on every wave; but it did plough along sedately at twelve miles per hour, was stable and completely reliable. We christened her the *June Bug* and she served us well.

That summer I also acquired a motley dog-team. They were a bunch of misfits but gradually they developed into a working team. Paddy, the lead dog, was mostly Alsatian. He never pulled his weight in his life. His traces were always slack but he obeyed every command given to him.

Brindle was mostly hound. He had been badly treated as a pup and snapped at everybody and everything within reach. We had to keep him in a muzzle before putting his harness on. The local people were terrified of him, which proved to be a blessing. Whenever we met another team on the trail, they always pulled well over and gave us a wide berth. We stopped for nothing.

Gwen, our third dog, was mostly Saint Bernard. We named her Gwen after a cartoon we saw in the newspaper, depicting an elegant dowager lady taking her tiny Pekinese for a walk; the caption read, 'Mush, Gwendolyn, mush.'

Brownie, the wheel dog, was a great, gentle beast, mostly collie. Tremendously strong, he loved to get into his harness. Brownie and Gwen were allowed to run loose so the tourists could photograph them, but Paddy and Brindle were kept chained up. Bea loved having the dogs around but hated cooking up the pails of food for them — cornmeal mush and crackling — every day.

Poor Brownie worshipped Gwen. Every once in a while she would lead him away into the bush, walking sedately while he frolicked around her. Then we would hear frantic barking and eventually the two of them would reappear, Gwen looking very smug and Brownie's face bristling with porcupine quills. Then followed a long and exhausting operation. Brownie had to be tied down and a broomstick jammed into his jaws to keep his mouth open. One by one, the porcupine quills had to be pulled out with a pair of pliers. Brownie never did learn. He continually followed Gwen into the bush, anticipating fun and games, and always ended up in the same sad condition.

Slowly the summer passed. While we were happy to see the

summer visitors when they arrived, by the end of the season, we were equally glad to see the back of them. I had promised the fur trade commissioner that I would make a go of Temagami and I was determined to do so. To ensure that the business always ran smoothly, I didn't take any time off at all. Our American customers were, on the whole, delightful people to deal with. They knew what they wanted and were willing to pay for it. But they wanted service and they expected it — *now*. When they wanted to talk to the 'Factor', as they insisted on calling me, they expected to deal with me personally, not an assistant.

The store opened at 8 a.m. and closed at 10 p.m., seven days a week. And I was always available. I ate and slept in that store. Bea didn't see much of me that first year, but she never complained. In later years, I changed the hours so that we were open from 9 a.m. to 9 p.m. on weekdays and from noon to 3 p.m. on Sundays. The changes sat well with our customers and we didn't seem to lose any sales.

With the arrival of fall, the tourists departed and the store hours were shortened from 9 a.m. to 6 p.m. on weekdays, except Fridays, when we stayed open for the mail. Blissfully, we closed all day on Sunday. By this time my apprentice, Art Howarth, had acquired enough knowledge to look after the store occasionally, while I took the odd afternoon off. Bea and I enjoyed these mild fall days; boating on the lake, fishing or just having a picnic lunch on a distant shore. On Sundays, we visited our friends who operated the various tourist camps around the lake.

When the weather turned colder and the deer-hunting season opened, I frequently went on hunting trips with several of the local men. Johnny Smallboy usually supervised the hunting expeditions. He'd take his big boat with six or eight of the Bay's rental canoes tied behind it and the bunch of us would set off. We would locate a large island or long peninsula where Johnny would choose a spot and put two men ashore. When the men were all in position, he turned his Kentucky beagle loose. As the dog picked up the scent of the deer, we heard his loud bugling as he took off in pursuit. We kept our positions to get a shot at the deer before it jumped into the water in an attempt to swim to safety on the mainland. We only had time for one quick shot once the deer exploded from the bush into the water. If the animal was only wounded and succeeded in making it to the water, we quickly paddled the canoe after it to finish it off. This type of hunting was perfectly legal in Ontario at this time. The local people were allowed to hunt for meat in season, the only provision being that when the day's hunting was over, the bag should not exceed more than one deer per person.

It dawned on me that on these excursions, I was always positioned in unusual spots. I suspected that my companions thought I wasn't a very good shot and placed me where I could do the least damage. While I was absolutely useless with a shotgun and ducks were always safe with me, I was better with a 30.30 rifle. I could let off a quick snap shot at a running deer and always hit it, providing it came my way, of course. And so far that hadn't happened. The first deer that came out near me, I killed cleanly with one shot. Having proved myself, I noticed that I was now placed in more favourable positions.

One memorable day, Johnny Smallboy and I were at either end of a narrow isthmus about a hundred yards wide, connecting a peninsula to the mainland. We could hear the hound bugling in full chase, but nothing seemed to come our way. About fifteen minutes later, I sensed rather than saw a gray shape moving quietly through the scrub about fifty yards away. I took a quick shot. Johnny came running over shouting, 'Did you get something?'

'I don't know, but I'm sure something moved over there. Let's go and see.' Sure enough, a fine buck was lying on the ground, stone dead. Johnny examined it carefully, then he looked up at me. 'But where did you hit it? I can't see any bullet wound.' We turned it over, examined it again and could find no bullet hole in the skin.

'Maybe it died of fright,' he said, laughing uproariously.

When the rest of the gang joined us, we hauled the buck out and suspended it from a tree to gralloch it. Johnny shouted for me to come over. 'Look at this. You shot it right up the rear end.' The bullet had travelled along just under the backbone and ended up against its shoulder blade. The Indians thought this was hilarious.

'I always knew you were a Scotsman, Mr Ross,' said Johnny

Ontario Archives

Johnny Smallboy with his wife and child. The daughter of former store manager S. R. Thorpe, sits on the porch. c. 1925.

chuckling quietly, 'but I didn't know you were as tight as all that. Fancy waiting until the deer turned its backside to you before you shot it, just so you wouldn't have a bullet hole in its hide.' This story went all around the territory and I was twitted unmercifully.

After freeze-up, Art asked me if he could make the regular weekly trip to Temagami with the dogs. Remembering how I had felt about taking the team on a trip when I was an apprentice clerk, I readily agreed. For the first few trips I sent a man along with him until he was thoroughly familiar with all the trails. For the rest of the winter, Art made this trip, week in and week out. On occasion, he would be late in returning if the going was tough or, especially at Christmas time, when the incoming mail was heavy. Several times he admitted that his rear end was trailing the ground by the time he reached the post, but he always made it. Art was a reliable dog handler and a good man on the trail.

*   *   *

During the summer, Bea had told me that we were going to have a child. We were both overjoyed and I insisted that she go down to Temagami regularly to see Dr McGowan. He found her to be in good physical condition and didn't expect any problems.

When the clique of little old ladies, led by Maggie Moore, heard the news, they bombarded us with advice. The baby was due to be born towards the end of January and the doctor recommended that Bea have the child at home. All we had to do was to telephone him when she started labour and he would drive across the ice to our house immediately. This sounded perfectly feasible and we agreed.

We fixed up a nursery and painted it in pastel colours. Bea spent the evenings knitting and sewing up small garments. Her parents were delighted at the news and parcels started to arrive from Winnipeg with alarming regularity: diapers, a layette, sweaters and even a crib and highchair. We received some beautifully knitted garments from my mother but her gifts were vastly outnumbered by the flow of parcels from Winnipeg. 'Your folks must think we're having triplets, with all the things they are sending,' I said.

In mid-January, we had one of those unexpected changes of weather and were hit by a heavy thaw. Dr McGowan called on the phone and said 'I don't like the look of the weather. I'm getting worried about your wife. She's getting very close to her time and if this mild spell continues, I won't be able to drive up the lake.' This had been worrying us too, so I asked him what he would suggest.

'The railway company has spotted a Red Cross hospital car at the village with a nurse in charge. You get your wife here as soon as possible, where we can look after her until the child is born.'

I agreed to send Bea down the following day. Just how I was going to get her there I couldn't imagine. And, like many a new father before me, I panicked. I couldn't leave the store. I decided the only thing to do was to consult with Granny Turner. After I had explained the problem, she said soothingly, 'Now, now, everything will be all right. Women have been having babies for a long time now. If the worst comes to the worst, we have a midwife here to take care of Mrs Ross. But I think we can get your wife down to the village safely.' She sat and thought for a couple of minutes. 'I think my son, Johnny Smallboy, should go along with your clerk to see that everything is okay. You have a cup of tea, while I go and find him.' And she rushed out the door.

In a few minutes she and Johnny returned. Granny looked at my worried face, put her hands on my shoulders and thrust me into a chair. 'Drink your tea, Mr Ross. There's nothing to be upset about.' And she and Johnny proceeded to explain how they were going to transport my very pregnant wife to Temagami village in the middle of January during a thaw.

Early next morning, the convoy set out with Johnny in the lead with his dog-team and Art following with ours. Each team pulled a jumper sleigh with a canoe securely lashed to it. Johnny sat in his canoe atop the sleigh, driving his dogs. Bea, cocooned in rugs and Hudson's Bay blankets, lay in the canoe on top of Art's sleigh, while he ran along behind. He was petrified at the thought that she might go into labour before they got to the village. I hated the idea of having to stay behind to tend the store, but I knew that Art and Johnny were skilled drivers and would take every precaution.

They travelled on the ice and not through the bush, as the trail was rough and might cause some harm to Bea. Johnny went ahead and picked out the trail and Art followed behind.

As they went slowly across the ice, they encountered a series of wide cracks with open water stretching right across the arm of the lake. They unhitched the dogs. Johnny paddled his canoe with the sleigh attached across to the other side. Then the dogs were swum across, hauled up on the ice and Johnny paddled back to do the same with Art's dogs.

With Bea still lying in the canoe, Art paddled it and his sleigh across the open water. Then they hitched up the dogs again and continued their slow trek over the miles to Temagami.

I spent a long, nail-biting morning in the store. Maggie Moore and her cronies kept vigil with me, constantly assuring me that Johnny Smallboy wouldn't let anything happen to Bea. Finally, Dr McGowan called to say that the party had arrived safely and Bea was in the hospital car.

Johnny and Art got back that evening with their dogs tired

and soaking wet and their harnesses coated with ice. They said the trip out had been risky, but it had worked out. They wouldn't want to try it a second time.

When I asked Bea about the trip later, she didn't seem to remember too much about it. 'As a matter of fact,' she said, 'I slept most of the way, I was so nice and warm.'

Every day, I called the hospital car, morning and evening. And each day, I received the same exasperating reply, 'Your wife is fine but nothing is happening yet.' I grew to hate that unctuous voice.

On the morning of 24 January, I made my usual call at nine o'clock. 'Mr Ross, the doctor took your wife by car to Cobalt about one o'clock this morning,' the nurse said. 'Didn't you know?' I was a bit short with her and asked why the move had taken place. 'Dr McGowan is worried about complications, so he decided that the hospital would be the best place for her.'

'What complications?' I yelled. She superciliously advised me that she wasn't privy to the doctor's reasons and suggested that I call him at the hospital.

After hearing this, I was frantic. I yelled to Art to hitch up the dog-team while I changed into travelling gear.

'I'm going to Cobalt. They've taken Bea there.' I thrust the keys of the post at him. 'You take charge until I get back.' I said, as I rushed out the door.

I'm willing to bet that the dogs never made a faster trip to Temagami. They seemed to sense the urgency and pulled as they never had before.

At the village, I chained up the dogs at the fire rangers' camp, made arrangements for them to be looked after, and called a taxi to drive me the sixty miles north to Cobalt. When the taxi dropped me in front of the hospital, I bumped into Dr McGowan. I was almost incoherent as I bombarded him with questions. 'How is my wife? What complications? Can I see her?' I asked. He put his arm around my shoulders and said, 'Slow down, Hugh. I brought Bea here because I thought if, and I say again, *if*, any complications arise, this is the best place for her. Let's go over to the hotel.' I was reluctant to go. I wanted to see for myself that Bea was all right.

He reassured me. 'Your wife is quite comfortable and her labour is coming along nicely. But these things take time and you can't rush nature. Nothing much is happening just now. That's why I'm going to have some lunch.'

We ambled over to the hotel and while I pushed the meat and potatoes around on the plate, unable to eat, Dr McGowan chattered away, trying to take my mind off everything that was happening. Realizing I was still very worried, he took me up to his room, poured me a drink and ordered me to drink it. Then he took me over to the window which overlooked the main street. Pointing, he indicated two buildings across the street. 'Do you see the bank and the drugstore over there?' As I nodded, he continued. 'I have one or two things to do. I'm going to the bank first and then to the drugstore. I want you to stay here until I get back. If a phone call comes through from the hospital, I'll be at one or the other of those two places. You come and let me know.' With that, he picked up his black bag and left.

I sat and paced and waited. The bank closed. Then the drugstore closed. Dr McGowan didn't return. The telephone didn't ring. I didn't dare leave in case the phone rang, so I just paced the floor. I was almost at the end of my tether when the phone rang at six-thirty. 'Congratulations, Hugh. You have a lovely, healthy daughter,' he boomed. It was 24 January 1939. 'Bea is sleeping and you can't see her right now.' As I started to ask the million questions that had been worrying me, he interrupted. 'I'll be at the hotel shortly and I'll tell you all about it.' I sagged with relief. Bea was all right and the baby was born safely.

When the doctor arrived and gave me the details, I realized just how difficult the birth had been. Dr McGowan had purposefully ditched me at the hotel so he wouldn't have a frantic husband running around the hospital making a nuisance of himself. It had been an instrument birth and at one time, the doctor hadn't been sure if he would lose the baby or the mother or both.

'Bea had a more difficult time than we expected and she'll take a few days to recover. But believe me, they are both just fine now,' he assured me. 'I think Bea had better stay here in the hospital for a few days. Then we'll get her down to the Red Cross railway car at Temagami for another few days.' Seeing I was alarmed again, he quickly added, 'It's just to make sure your wife is perfectly well before she and the baby go home with you. Let's say in about two weeks.'

He agreed that I could go over to the hospital the next morning to take a peek at my new daughter. She was a lovely little thing with pale golden hair. Bea looked very tired but triumphant as she cuddled the baby. 'Well, honey, have you decided on her name?' I asked. We had discussed names during the long winter evenings but had made no firm decision.

'Barbara Jane,' she said, looking down at the small bundle in her arms. 'We'll call her Barbara Jane Ross.' We spent a little time together, counting fingers and toes, and too soon, it was time for me to leave.

I thanked Dr McGowan for his kindness, called a taxi and drove the sixty miles south to Temagami. There I hitched up my dog-team and went back to the post.

The store was full of people. Suspecting that some calamity had occurred while I was away, I pushed anxiously through the crowd. 'What's the matter, Art? What are all these people doing here?'

Art laughed. 'Boss, you went out of here in an awful hurry yesterday and we hadn't heard from you since. So everyone is here waiting to hear how things are and whether your wife had a boy or a girl.' Greatly relieved, I turned to the gathering and announced that Barbara Jane Ross had been born on 24 January and mother and daughter were doing well.

'But,' I added, wearily, 'I'm not too sure about the father.'

Fortunately, during the following two weeks, the thaw ended and Dr McGowan was able to drive Bea and the baby home.

What a difference the arrival of a baby makes to a household. Our every move had to be planned around her schedule. Until she was older, we couldn't just pick up and go for a walk in the bush as we had been accustomed to doing. Both of us played second fiddle to the baby, and I was soon participating in the sacred rites of bathing, changing and feeding Barbara. Everywhere I looked, there seemed to be diapers drying. There weren't any disposable diapers, so every day was washday — and the water all had to be brought up from the lake. To help Bea with the increased work, I hired George Turner's daughter, Isabel.

The 1939 summer season was hectic as usual, and there was a lot of talk among the summer visitors about Adolf Hitler who was making belligerent noises in Europe. Then in September, England and Canada declared war on Germany.

*   *   *

Art was transferred to Dinorwic in the fall. Bea and I were truly sorry to see him go. He was a first-class assistant and had become almost a member of our family. I then hired George Turner's son, Robert who was known as Boychee, to help me in the store and carry the winter mail.

In the summer of 1940, I met my first movie star. Sterling McNees from Pittsburgh had a summer lodge and he brought his guests, the Stewarts, over to meet us. Mrs Stewart had a problem. She wanted to go out fishing but was afraid to go out in a small boat. Donald McKenzie, who was guiding for Mr McNees, suggested that they talk to me about hiring the *June Bug*. I readily agreed to this plan, as Mr McNees was a friend and a valued customer.

'You must meet my son, Jimmy,' said Mrs Stewart. I must have looked vague, for I didn't have a clue who Jimmy Stewart was. 'He's in the movie business,' she added. When I still didn't react, she announced, 'He's a famous movie star.' I said that I would be delighted to meet her son and excused myself. I went into the office, cornered Glen Maconnell and asked, 'Who the hell is Jimmy Stewart? His mother is out there and thinks I should know who her son is. I haven't seen a film since 1935. Who is he?' Glen filled me in and armed with this information, I went back into the store. 'Come outside and meet Jimmy,' she urged. We found him still on the dock, busily taking snapshots of my two husky pups which I had imported the previous spring from Moose Factory. The pups were young and playful and allowed to run loose. I planned to breed a dog-team, a proper dog-team, eventually.

Mrs Stewart introduced me to a very tall, good-looking, quiet, young man to whom I took an instant liking. Bea and I were invited over to the lodge to have dinner with them several times. Bea, of course, had known all about Jimmy Stewart and was as charmed by him as I was.

Mr Stewart, Sr. was in the hardware business so he frequently came over to the store to inspect the stock. He was an avid collector of antiques and when he saw the old Indian pipe which I had been given by Alex Foubister at Grassy Narrows, he fell in love with it and persuaded me to part with it. He refused to accept it as a gift so we dickered back and forth, both of us enjoying the haggling, until we agreed on a price for the pipe and an old door lock that I had picked up somewhere along the line. His son, however, was convinced his dad had taken advantage of me in the deal. Later on in the year, he sent me a glossy photograph inscribed 'From the son of the guy who stole an Indian pipe from you.' I still have that picture on my wall.

That summer we were looking forward to the birth of our second child in early October. This time we were making sure that there would be no repetition of the trouble prior to Barbara's birth. So in late August, Bea and Barbara (who was a delight, walking around with a cloud of that fine, pale, gold hair) went into Winnipeg to stay with Bea's parents. I had accumulated a lot of holiday time, so I arranged to go to the city the third week in September.

Our second daughter, Jennifer Ann, was born in Grace Hospital in Winnipeg on 3 October 1940. She was lovely, looked very much like her mother, but was as dark-haired as Barbara was fair. It was a normal birth and eleven days later we returned to Temagami, flying by Trans Canada Airways to North Bay. Jennifer must have been one of their youngest passengers ever.

Shortly after we returned, I was approached by Dr McGowan and Jack Sproat who owned the Temagami Boat Company. They had a proposition for me. Herb Lloyd, who owned and operated a large general store and post office in Temagami village, wanted to retire and sell his business. Dr McGowan and Jack Sproat proposed to put up the capital to buy the business and wanted me to operate it. All the profits would be split three

Jimmy Stewart, who inscribed this photograph: 'From the son of the guy who stole an Indian pipe from you.'

ways. After discussing it with Bea, I turned it down. The possibilities of making a good living were there, but I had a secure job with the Company with excellent chances for further promotion. Moreover, I was now a family man with two young daughters and I couldn't convince myself that it was a good time to make changes. If I took this job, it would mean that we would stay in Temagami for the rest of our lives — and I still had gypsy feet and a wandering spirit.

The following summer, a representative of a film company called in to see me. They were making a movie near New Liskeard, a town about seventy miles north of Temagami.

'Mr Ross,' said the nattily dressed representative, 'I understand that you own a dog-team.'

'That's right, I do,' I replied, wondering why anyone would
want a dog-team in the summertime.

'I suppose you know all about the film.' When I indicated
that I didn't, he went on to explain. 'What we need is a dog-team
for a short sequence in the film, and we'd like to know if we can
rent the team for a few days' shooting.'

The team was just lying around during the summer, eating
cornmeal mush and getting fat, so I agreed that they could hire
them. 'Providing,' I added, 'that I can send along an Indian to
look after the dogs and see that they are properly fed. Of course,
you will have to pay the guide's wages as well as for the food for
the team.' That is great, I thought. I might even make a bob or two
on the deal. I looked at the man to see how he was taking all these
stipulations, but he never batted an eyelid.

'That's fine, Mr Ross. We'll take care of the dogs and the
Indian and see that they are fed. Now, down to business.' He sort
of squared his shoulders as if he expected a long battle. 'How
much do you want to rent the dogs?'

I thought it over, figured out how much it cost to feed the
dogs and said in a firm voice, '$15.00'. I hoped he wasn't going to
bargain, but I was prepared to lower the price by another ten per
cent.

'Done,' he agreed with alacrity. We shook hands and made
arrangements for delivery of the dogs to the location site.

The company was making a war film about bush pilots who
were recruited to the Royal Canadian Air Force to ferry bombers
across from Canada to Great Britain. It was entitled 'Captains of
the Clouds' and starred James Cagney. To my disappointment,
the dogs appeared in the film for all of 20 seconds, when a bush
plane drew up to a trading-post dock and a trapper emerged
leading the dogs out of the plane.

When the dogs were returned, the film company's representative thanked me and handed me a cheque. I glanced at it and put
it in my pocket. Then realizing what I had read, I pulled it out
again. Instead of the $15.00 that I had agreed to, the cheque was

Beatrice Ross with Barbara Jane, in front of the Temagami Store.

made out for $15.00 per dog, per day. I thanked him again, and this time I really meant it.

More of my holiday time had mounted up, and in mid-September 1941, we took the children to visit their grandparents in Winnipeg. The girls were growing by leaps and bounds and the grandparents hadn't seen them since Jennifer was eleven days old.

We had enjoyed about three weeks of our visit — to the delight of the grandparents and the despair of Bea and me, for they were spoiling the children rotten — when the phone rang one morning. Head Office wanted to see me immediately.

Mr Parsons had retired and was replaced by Robert Chesshire who had the title of general manager of the fur trade department. Mr Chesshire wasted no time in coming straight to the point. A district manager in Montreal was seriously ill and they were transferring T. D. Lindley, the post manager at Waterways in northern Alberta, to his position. Would I take over for Mr Lindley? I was agreeable, but asked for time to discuss the move with my wife.

Mr Chesshire pointed to the telephone. 'Call her now,' he

said. 'I need to have an answer immediately. If she agrees, you will have to leave for the west tomorrow.'

Almost in shock, I protested. 'But we are only here on holiday. All we have are the clothes we have with us. What about our personal belongings? Our furniture? I would have to go back to Temagami to pack everything up.'

'I'm sorry, but there's no time for that now,' said Mr Chesshire. 'We'll take care of that for you. We have a good man we can send to Temagami. He'll look after everything.'

We discussed the logistics of the move and then he said, 'We will send you back to Temagami later on in the spring to pack up. You can tell Mrs Ross that we are building a new house at Waterways, complete with all modern conveniences and it will be furnished by the Company, right down to the last teaspoon.'

So I phoned Bea and once she got over the shock, she agreed. 'It's not like we have a choice, is it? Oh well, I knew what I was getting into when I married you. But sometimes I feel like a fireman. The bell rings and we're off.'

Later, as we pored over a map of Alberta, Bea asked if we would have a dog-team. When I shook my head no, she heaved a great sigh. 'Thank God, I'll never have to cook up a pail of cornmeal mush again!'

Next morning, 4 November 1941, the four of us caught the train to Waterways to see what the west had in store for us. But that's another story.

*   *   *

I was a member of the Company of Adventurers of England Trading into Hudson's Bay from 1930 to 1977. We were posted to many places and have seen many changes. Dog-teams and canoes are no longer used for transportation, but for recreation. Life may be easier now, but ours was a gentler time, when the people were important.

Never, in all the forty-seven years I spent with the Company did I have to steer a course by the stars in an open boat. And in all that time, I never had to ride a bareback horse.

INDEX